D1251581

KOREA, JUNE 1871 THE
TRESPASSERS

KOREA, JUNE 1871 THE TRESPASSERS

by Irving Werstein

ILLUSTRATED BY JOSEPH PAPIN

E. P. DUTTON & CO., INC.   *New York*

This book is for Goldie and Jack, with love.

WAR ON THE ONE HAND IS SUCH A TERRIBLE, SUCH AN ATROCIOUS THING, THAT NO MAN, ESPECIALLY NO CHRISTIAN MAN, HAS THE RIGHT TO ASSUME THE RESPONSIBILITY OF BEGINNING IT. . . .

COUNT LEO TOLSTOY, *Anna Karenina,*
Part VIII, Chapter 15.

AUTHOR'S NOTE

In *The Trespassers,* I have attempted to re-create an obscure episode in American history, a forgotten dark moment, when the United States became involved in an unsavory incident which was quickly hidden under piles of official red tape.

My purpose in illuminating this occurrence is to show my young readers that even a great nation like this can be guilty of mistaken judgment; that even a democracy can behave like a bully.

It is interesting to note that the scene of this incident was Korea, a land which has figured largely in recent history. It is also interesting that in the case of the U.S.S. *Pueblo*, the United States acted with forbearance and patience, not as it did on that distant day in June 1871.

In retelling the story of the Battle of Kanghwa Island, I have occasionally added plausible supposition and some dialogue. However, remarks made by historical personages are taken verbatim as contained in official documents. Correspondence and reports are authentic.

I was aided immeasurably in my research by the Naval History Division, Office of the Chief of Naval Operations, especially F. Kent Loomis, Captain, USN (Ret.), Assistant Director of Naval History.

The librarians of the New-York Historical Society and the American History Room of the New York Public Library were most helpful.

As always, Chip Chafetz and Sid Solomon of the noted Pageant Book Store on lower Fourth Avenue in New York City dug deeply into their treasure trove of out-of-print material. I thank them heartily.

I thank my agent, Miss Candida Donadio, for her splendid suggestions; my wife for her patience; and my son, Jack, for steering clear when the working lamp was lit.   —*I.W.*

NEW YORK, MARCH 1969

CONTENTS

11

KOREA, JUNE 1871 THE
TRESPASSERS

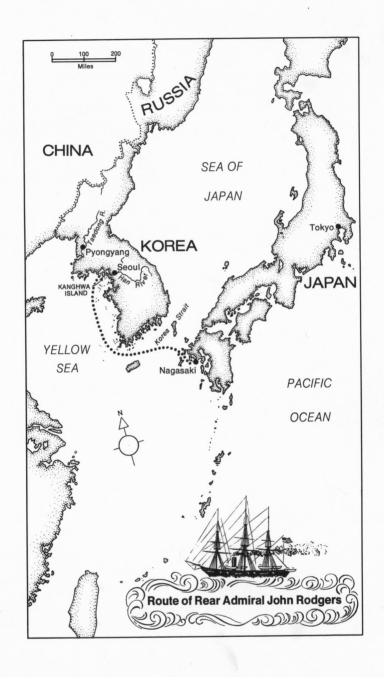

Route of Rear Admiral John Rodgers

THE LAND OF THE MORNING CALM

IN 1866 THE COUNTRY THEN KNOWN BY ITS ANCIENT
name, Chosen, which lay on a peninsula 600 miles
long and 135 miles wide, jutting down from Man-
churia between Japan and China, had been shut off
from the outside world for centuries. Also known
as the Hermit Kingdom and the Land of the Morning Calm, this mysterious nation had yet another
name—Korea.

Ruled by an absolute monarch, Chosen, or Korea,
was nominally a tributary of China; but not even

that arrangement could disturb the isolation of the Hermit Kingdom.

Neither did the entry of European maritime powers and the United States into the Orient during the nineteenth century alter the Korean *status quo*. The only inroads by foreigners had been made by a handful of Roman Catholic missionaries who had set up schools and converted some of the Buddhist natives to Catholicism.

Aside from the missionaries, Koreans had little or no contact with outsiders. The sole aliens who traveled freely to Chosen and back were Chinese traders. Through the centuries other people had trespassed upon Korean soil, but never remained for long. The Mongols overran the country in the thirteenth century. However, their reign was brief. After a few decades, the Mongols left, and Chosen returned once more to its own sequestered tranquillity.

Left to themselves, the Koreans proved to be an ingeniously inventive people. In 1392 a powerful dynasty, the Yi, rose to power and dominated the country. During the course of the Yi regime, the Koreans developed metal movable printing type, preceding Gutenberg by more than fifty years. They also made astronomical instruments of a high order and created other mechanical innovations decades before their counterparts were known in Europe and elsewhere.

At the end of the sixteenth century, in the year 1592, a Japanese general named Hideyoshi believed that it was his destiny to conquer the known world. As the first step in this ambitious project, he invaded Chosen with 300,000 troops armed with matchlocks, a crude type of firearm. The Koreans had nothing to equal this weapon, and Hideyoshi's forces triumphed everywhere.

Indeed, so demoralized were the Koreans that they offered little or no opposition to the conquering general. However, Yisunsin, a noble Korean admiral, checkmated Hideyoshi. Yisunsin, a relative of the ruling dynasty, was a man of many talents—an artist, sculptor, musician, and inventor—a Korean Leonardo da Vinci. His first love was the sea and ships; he had designed many sailing vessels over the years and, with the Japanese spreading across his country, turned his mind to ways of defeating the invader.

The foe's weakness lay in the fact that he had to supply his armies in Korea by ship. At regular intervals Japanese convoys sailed from the home islands to Chosen, always escorted by the Imperial Navy. Yisunsin decided to sever this Nipponese lifeline.

He designed and built a unique warship, the first ironclad in history. It was known as the Tortoise

Boat because of a huge hinged iron shell that covered the craft like a lid, thus keeping the enemy from boarding or burning the vessel.

Sporting a fierce dragon's head bowsprit, the Tortoise Boat, which was propelled by oars, mounted crude cannon. (Although they lacked individual firearms, the Koreans had long known about gunpowder and had primitive types of artillery.) The impregnable Tortoise Boat waddled into one of Hideyoshi's convoys in the Sea of Japan and destroyed the entire fleet.

Inspired by their victory at sea, the Koreans rallied. Aided by a Chinese army that was equipped with better matchlocks than the Japanese had, they drove the Nipponese invaders from their soil. It was this sixteenth-century intervention in Korea by China that started the long-drawn-out enmity between the Japanese and the Chinese.

Although rid of Hideyoshi, the Koreans were not done with foreign interlopers. They were next invaded by their erstwhile Chinese allies. In 1627 Manchu armies from China fell upon Chosen and quickly humbled the Hermit Kingdom. However, the Manchus proved to be rather amiable conquerors. They set no harsh regimen over the Koreans, exacted minimal tribute, and made no attempt to impose Chinese ways upon their subjects.

In the nineteenth century, although China had been opened up to European nations and the Americans, Prince Tai-Wun, the Yi ruler of Chosen, was permitted to keep his country in isolation. Under the Chinese, the Land of the Morning Calm remained almost unchanged.

For some reason, however, a rabid wave of antiforeignism engulfed Chosen in 1866. This antipathy assumed violent shape when the usually placable Koreans turned on the Roman Catholic missionaries who had been living among them for many years. In an outburst of senseless fury, a Korean mob swarmed through a Catholic mission near Seoul, burned the buildings, and killed nine French missionaries, among them, three nuns.

Word of this massacre was brought from Korea by Chinese traders. It reached the ears of French, German, British, and American businessmen in the ports of Woosing, Chefoo, and Shanghai. Great indignation was voiced in the foreign enclaves. There was much talk of "doing something about it" and "teaching those heathens a lesson." However, nothing concrete took place, although the French moved some warships to Chinese and Japanese bases.

That same year, only a month or so after the slaying of the Catholics, the *Surprise*, an American merchant schooner, was wrecked off the coast of the

Hermit Kingdom, some miles northwest of Seoul.

The survivors managed to reach the rocky shore in lifeboats. Instead of harming them, the Koreans treated the mariners as honored guests. A message was carried to the American consul at Shanghai that the men of the *Surprise* were receiving good care and would be returned to China by the first vessel available. After two weeks, the sailors arrived at Shanghai looking healthy, well fed, and laden with gifts and souvenirs of their stay in Chosen.

The treatment accorded the Americans seemed to indicate that the antiforeign tide had receded in Korea. However, observers were even more puzzled by what happened to another American ship just a short time after the *Surprise* incident.

On September 11, 1866, the merchant schooner *General Sherman,* many weeks out of her home port of Boston, Massachusetts, took on a cargo of assorted merchandise at Chefoo and sailed across the Yellow Sea to Korea.

Captain Matthias Bledsoe, the skipper of the *General Sherman,* was a veteran of the China trade. He wanted to do business with the Koreans and was determined to do so despite the ban on foreigners imposed by Prince Tai-Wun.

Three days later, the *General Sherman* reached the headwaters of the Taedong River in northern

Korea and started for the city of Pyongyang. After proceeding only a few miles, the *General Sherman* was hailed by local officials, who came out on the river in junks and ordered Captain Bledsoe to leave at once. He paid no heed to them and pushed on upstream.

During the morning of September 15, the river level fell suddenly. This was not unusual in the early autumn and happened to many Korean rivers. With the river down, the *General Sherman* grounded in the mud and stuck fast.

No clear picture of what happened next is known. The account most generally accepted alleged that when the ship went aground, Korean villagers tried to board the mired vessel but were beaten off by the *General Sherman's* crew.

The Koreans then fashioned shallow-draft fire rafts, floated them down the river, and set the wooden schooner afire. The American sailors abandoned their blazing ship, only to be captured by the villagers and beaten to death.

Most versions of the *General Sherman's* fate differ only slightly from this one. The major disagreement has to do with the crew. Some claimed that only the officers were put to death, while the ordinary seamen were imprisoned at Pyongyang. However, another story had all the ship's company herded across the

Manchurian border and set loose in that rugged region without proper food or clothing. If this were the case, all must have perished.

No matter what befell the *General Sherman's* sailors, unsettling reports reached the American consul general at Shanghai. It was clear to him that some sort of understanding had to be reached with the Hermit Kingdom concerning the treatment of shipwrecked sailors.

Neither the United States nor any other maritime power could permit their ships and merchant seamen to be endangered by the Koreans. With seaborne commerce to the Orient on the rise, the possibilities were good that other incidents, such as those involving the *Surprise* and the *General Sherman,* would take place.

But the Seoul authorities rebuffed all attempts to reach a settlement. Indeed, Prince Tai-Wun refused to acknowledge receipt of any communications. As far as he was concerned, the rest of the world did not exist.

The loss of the *General Sherman* and possible massacre of her sailors aroused official wrath in Washington. So indignant was Secretary of State William H. Seward that he proposed to the French ambassador a plan to take joint action against the Koreans for the purpose of "obtaining satisfaction and to

punish those who wantonly murdered nationals of our countries. . . ."

The French turned down Seward. They were eager to become the dominant power in the Orient and wanted no joint ventures there. If any flag was going to fly in Korean waters, it would be the tricolor of France.

Barely a dozen years had passed since Japan and China had opened their ports for trade. The lucrative Oriental markets were still "up for grabs." Although the United States had paved the way into Japan in 1853 with a squadron of warships flying the Stars and Stripes and commanded by Commodore Matthew Perry, the French felt that working with the Americans would not be advantageous to them.

Having rebuffed Seward, the French went ahead with a unilateral move against the Koreans. In mid-October 1866 a flotilla of seven French warships entered the swift waters of the Han River and headed up toward Seoul, the capital of the Hermit Kingdom.

The French ships, under the command of Rear Admiral Pierre Gustav Rozé, sailed unimpeded to Kanghwa, a fortified island several miles downriver from Seoul. Known as the Gibraltar of Chosen, Kanghwa was swarming with troops manning the forts that guarded the approaches to the capital city. Although an estimated five thousand Koreans were on the island, Rozé sent ashore a force of only two hundred marines after conducting a haphazard bombardment of the forts. When the first salvos crashed upon them, the Koreans abandoned the forts and retreated out of naval gun range.

Once Rozé's marines had landed and the ships had to hold their fire, the Koreans came roaring back. The invaders were overwhelmed by the savage charge of the Koreans. While fighting raged on Kanghwa, dozens of fire rafts were floated downstream on the ebb tide. These incendiary vessels imperiled the wooden warships and made it difficult for Admiral Rozé to keep his flotilla on station.

Made rudely aware that his expedition was in grave jeopardy, Rozé ordered the landing party, or what was left of it, to withdraw. He laid down a covering barrage so that the marines could get off the beach and return to the ships in the boats that had carried them to Kanghwa. Thoroughly whipped, they suffered heavy losses in dead and wounded. Once the survivors of the ill-fated force had embarked on the warships, Rozé pulled out.

The French defeat brought frenzied rejoicing in Seoul. Crowds gathered outside the palace to serenade Prince Tai-Wun and to hail General Wo-Pei, who had commanded the soldiers on Kanghwa. Three days of public feasting was declared. Everywhere in Chosen, the slogan "Death to Foreigners!" was painted on buildings, walls, and fences.

So pleased was Prince Tai-Wun by the victory at Kanghwa that he promoted all officers and gave a monetary present to every man who had helped defend the island. For Wo-Pei, there was a special honor. The Prince had a medal struck off to commemorate the victory of Kanghwa and on one side of it ordered Wo-Pei's likeness engraved.

Rozé's defeat was a blow to France. Not only had he failed to get "satisfaction" for the slaying of the missionaries, but the occurrence had turned Chosen still further against the outside world. More than ever before, the Hermit Kingdom was living up to its name.

2 "THOSE PEOPLE HAVE NO HEART..."

HAVING SEEN THE HUMILIATION OF THE FRENCH BY the Koreans, the Americans decided to make their own overtures to the Seoul government. The screw-sloop *Wachusett*, under Commander Robert W. Shufeldt, steamed up the Han River in December 1866. (A screw-sloop was a sailing vessel equipped with auxiliary steam-powered engines.)

Shufeldt made it obvious that he was not on a warlike mission. From foremast and stern he flew the Stars and Stripes with huge white flags of truce affixed to the halyards beneath them.

Tarpaulins covered his guns, and he had a small fife and drum band playing in the ship's bow. "If ever a vessel was made to appear unmartial, she was the *Wachusett*. . . . We started upriver rather like a Sunday School excursion boat instead of a man-of-war," a junior officer aboard the sloop noted in his journal.

Also on the *Wachusett* was an officer who spoke Chinese and Korean, to act as interpreter for Commander Shufeldt. In addition, the sloop carried a generous supply of tawdry baubles which were supposed to be handed out to Korean officials as a sign of goodwill.

"Somebody in the State Department apparently was under the misapprehension that we were going to parley with Sioux or Cheyenne chiefs out here," the diarist recorded. "We had an assortment of cheap watches, magnifying glasses, colored beads, and similar stuff to hand out. . . ."

Just below Kanghwa Island, the *Wachusett* was hailed by a passenger-carrying junk. After some talk back and forth, Shufeldt invited the Koreans aboard. The diary-keeping officer noted with amusement: "Onto the ship came five Korean officials clad in magnificently jeweled robes. . . . On their fingers sparkled golden rings set with precious stones. . . . The commander took one look and whispered, 'Forget the gifts! We've nothing they want!' . . . It would have been the rankest insult to offer our visitors the trash we had for them. . . ."

Politely, but firmly, the Koreans refused permission for Shufeldt to continue his voyage up the Han to Seoul. They would not even accept a message for the Prince. Nor, when questioned, would they say more about the *General Sherman* than the repeated assertion that the Americans had "brought on their own doom."

Commander Shufeldt could not even learn whether some of the men might still be alive. Since there was no point in continuing the conversation, he bade his visitors farewell and they took their departure.

The commander then held council with his officers. All agreed that it would be folly to proceed any farther upriver. The *Wachusett* was not armed heavily enough to shoot her way past the forts, and nothing could be gained by making such a foolhardy attempt.

Accordingly, the vessel swung about and returned to Chefoo, where Shufeldt delivered his report. The mission had been a dismal failure. The fate of the *General Sherman*'s crew remained a mystery although Shufeldt was convinced that all the men were dead.

However, from time to time came rumors that

some of them had survived. In May 1868 Rear Admiral Henry A. Ball, then commanding the United States Asiatic Fleet, which was based at Woosing, China, heard from a Chinese merchant recently back from Chosen that most of the *General Sherman*'s sailors still lived. According to the merchant, they were imprisoned north of the 38th parallel above Pyongyang.

Admiral Ball reacted quickly to this story. He dispatched Commander John C. Feibiger in the ironclad screw-sloop *Shenandoah* to run down the lead. An earnest, tough seadog, Feibiger was a veteran of many naval engagements in the Civil War. He sailed to Chosen with his ship stripped for action. No truce flags flew from the *Shenandoah*. Her guns were uncovered, loaded and manned, as she sailed into the mouth of the Taedong River on the way to Pyongyang.

Korean officials met the sloop before she had gone very far upriver. They were received without ceremony aboard the *Shenandoah*. Under questioning, they denied that the crewmen of the *General Sherman* were imprisoned near Pyongyang or anywhere in Korea. All of them were dead, they insisted.

Before leaving the sloop, the Koreans warned Feibiger to depart at once unless he wanted to risk his men and his ship. Through an interpreter, a

Korean said, "Be out of these waters before the sun sets or else prepare to die."

Commander John Feibiger was not a man easily bluffed or frightened. "Tell that clown I'll go when I'm ready to go and not a minute sooner," he growled at the interpreter. "Tell him that if he doesn't behave, we'll blast Pyongyang to rubble."

The Chinese who was acting as a go-between for the Americans had more tact than did the commander. His translation brought an unexpected response from the Koreans, who bowed graciously, grinned amicably, and clambered down the Jacob's ladder to their waiting junk with sunny smiles, waving farewell in the friendliest fashion.

Their conduct puzzled Feibiger. "Why were they so damned pleasant?" he asked the interpreter.

"Why not?" was the response. "One cannot see into the minds of other men. The ways of Orientals are inscrutable."

"Maybe so," Feibiger shrugged. "But we're not leaving yet. I'm going to take some soundings in these waters. You never can tell when we may be sailing in them again."

For the next two days, the *Shenandoah* steamed slowly along on a surveying mission. The river was charted, obstacles marked, depth soundings taken, the speed and direction of currents recorded.

On the third morning, as the sloop rounded a bend in the river, masked shore batteries opened fire on her. The *Shenandoah*'s bugler sounded "General Quarters." The sailors dashed to battle stations. For a while, it appeared as though the American ship would trade shots with the battery, but Feibiger withheld the order to open fire.

Standing on the quarterdeck, he gripped the railing and frowned in concentration. He had been given no orders to engage in hostilities with the Koreans, only to defend his ship if it were endanered.

Although shells of various calibers were whizzing by, they all splashed harmlessly into the Taedong, throwing up great geysers of river water. The *Shenandoah* remained unscathed by that hurricane of missiles. If he replied to the shore guns, Feibiger reasoned, he might well start an international incident which would go far beyond his jurisdiction.

"Right then, I decided that discretion was preferable to committing an act of indiscretion. I ordered the ship turned about," he later wrote. "If the Koreans had not put up such an exhibition of incredibly poor marksmanship and actually endangered my ship, I might have replied with everything I had. But, as it was, we couldn't have been safer cruising on the Potomac."

The *Shenandoah* put about slowly and deliberately, making a lazy circle in the river as the Korean gunners blazed away ineffectually.

"Were it not for the water thrown high by the shells, one might have supposed the shore batteries were using blanks," a *Shenandoah* sailor noted in his journal. "The only casualties that resulted from all the shooting were hundreds of fish killed by the detonations. They could be seen bobbling on the surface, carried along on the swift current. . . ."

As the *Shenandoah* pulled away, the shore gunners leaped and shouted for joy as though they had driven off the interloper. From somewhere a band appeared, complete with cymbals, drums, trumpets, and odd-shaped native instruments, to serenade the cannoneers.

Each man was personally congratulated by Prince Tai-Wun, who once more proclaimed a three-day-long festival to celebrate the defeat of "foreign devils."

"Of one thing your Highness may be certain," an adviser told the Prince. "Those people have no heart to face our tiger warriors. They will never again return. . . ."

THE UNITED STATES ASIATIC STATION 3

FOR SOME TIME IT LOOKED AS THOUGH THE PRINCE'S adviser had a gift of prophecy. There came no further encroachments on Chosen. The Hermit Kingdom remained shrouded in secrecy and mystery, although rumors and fanciful tales seeped out of the isolated Land of the Morning Calm.

In Chinese and Japanese waterfront dives frequented by sailors, many wild yarns were spun about the Hermit Kingdom and her people. Since very few Europeans, Americans, or any other Westerner, had

37

ever set foot in Chosen, even the most imaginative stories about that country were accepted by gullible listeners. Sailors who had never been near the place described the people of Korea as "gigantic in stature" and of "Herculean strength"; Koreans were said to have the "ferocity of tigers."

According to one "informant," the army of the Hermit Kingdom was equipped with deadly weapons "not yet known in the Western world." Prince Tai-Wun's soldiers, it was said, had "fanatical courage," and death held no terrors for them. To prove all this, had not the Koreans decimated a French force and beaten back an American warship?

Barroom experts claimed to know the reason for the jealously guarded seclusion of the Hermit Kingdom. It was gold! Fabulous hoards of gold! In the Korean hills, they said, the yellow stuff lay about on the surface. Every stream bed was lined with gold nuggets. Not only gold abounded, these sages declared, but also precious gems: diamonds, rubies, emeralds.

Chosen, they said, was rich beyond belief. Small wonder foreigners were excluded. Who could blame the Koreans for wanting to keep such wealth to themselves?

That these stories impressed ignorant sailors in sleazy grogshops was of little significance. But they were accepted as gospel by British, French, German, and American traders in China and Japan.

These avaricious men wanted a cut of the Korean treasure. They persistently demanded that their governments "do something" about opening up Chosen, that land of limitless wealth and untapped markets for Western goods.

That the Koreans did not choose to have dealings with outsiders did not seem to matter. Who cared what those heathen wanted? If the Koreans refused to open their portals to world trade and commerce, then the "civilized" nations must smash through the barriers.

By 1868 the clamoring of business interests over Korea was growing louder in Paris, London, Berlin, and Washington. More and more insistent became the outcries that "something must be done" about the Chosen impasse.

Rear Admiral Stephen C. Rowan, who had relieved Ball as commander of the United States Asiatic Fleet, advised Secretary of State William Seward that in his opinion "it would be beneficial for the United States to wrest a trade treaty from the ruler of Chosen . . . by any method, including force if need be. . . ."

Rowan outlined to Gideon Welles, the Secretary of the Navy, a plan for a naval expedition to Chosen, "which will have the same purposes and effects as Commodore Perry's squadron had upon Japan. . . ."

Influenced by the baseless reports of Korean military prowess, Rowan called for a fleet of frigates, sloops, and gunboats strong enough to mount a major campaign. He also requested a landing force of marines and bluejackets equipped with field artillery.

Welles was not convinced that the country could mount such an operation so soon after the Civil War. His tenure in office was reaching its conclusion, and a new administration would be taking over on March 4, 1869. Rather than make a decision on Rowan's proposal, Welles tabled it, reasoning that his successor could tackle the Chosen question should it arise again.

On January 1, 1870, Rear Admiral Rowan was relieved by Rear Admiral John Rodgers, who came from a family with a long naval tradition. His grandfather and father had been renowned officers in the United States Navy. Born in 1812, John Rodgers was a hearty and vigorous man of fifty-eight, who had followed the sea all his life.

At the time that he assumed command of what was officially designated the United States Asiatic Station, he took over a post that embraced "all the waters of Asia, Eastern and North Eastern Africa, and the islands of the Eastern Ocean."

It was a big mouthful for any man to swallow, but John Rodgers was equal to it. A crusty seadog, he had seen action in the war with Mexico and the Civil War. In the latter conflict, he had commanded the ironclad sloop *Weehawken.*

Under Rodgers, that doughty ship had participated in several important naval operations, including the capture of New Orleans, the Battle of Mobile Bay, blockade action in the Atlantic, and the bombardment of Fort Fisher, a Confederate bastion which had held out until the end of the war.

The country had a dynamic Secretary of the Navy, George Robeson, at the time Rodgers went to the Asiatic Station. A driving, progressive man, Robeson was determined that the United States would have a navy that, in his words, would be "second to none."

After the Civil War, the United States Navy had fallen into disrepair. Its ships, mostly obsolete wooden frigates, were inadequate for any but the most routine duties. The ironclads, which had done such splendid service in the war, lay rusting and corroding at navy yards from Brooklyn to New Orleans. Fewer than a dozen ships, which had been built late in the war, were adequate for the needs of a modern navy.

Secretary Robeson somehow managed to awaken Congress from its lethargy. He pushed through appropriations for the construction of ironclads rang-ing in size from frigate to gunboat. Robeson also wangled funds to modernize some ships in the active fleet.

Because he was a man with rare foresight, Robeson realized that the Asiatic Station was of prime importance to the interests of the United States. When Admiral Rodgers went to the Far East, the headquarters of the United States Asiatic Fleet was at Woosing, China. Coaling stations and naval bases had also been established at various places along the coasts of China and Japan.

Because Robeson had an interest in the Orient, several of the newest and best ships in the navy were assigned to Admiral Rodgers. These included the screw-frigate *Colorado* (Captain George H. Cooper), the flagship of the Asiatic Fleet; the screw-sloops *Alaska* (Commander Homer C. Blake) and *Benecia* (Commander Lewis A. Kimberley); the ironclad gunboat *Palos* (Lieutenant Commander Charles H. Rockwell); and the ironclad sidewheeler *Monocacy* (Commander E. P. McCrae). (The *Monocacy* was a "double-ender"—a type of vessel generally used as a ferryboat. Sheathed in iron and mounting batteries of 25-pounders, 18-pounders, and mortars, craft such as the *Monocacy* made potent bombardment ships. Her sister ship, the *Ashuelot*, was also earmarked for Rodgers, but could not join the fleet for some time because her engines had broken down and needed replacement.)

These vessels, several steam launches, a company of United States marines carried on the *Colorado* and the *Benecia,* and about six hundred sailors comprised Rodgers' command. His flotilla had nearly one hundred guns of various calibers, some artillery fieldpieces, and an arsenal of small weapons, such as breech-loading rifles for the bluejackets and leathernecks who might be deployed as landing parties.

Sailing aboard the *Colorado,* Rodgers left the United States late in 1869. The ship had a fine voyage from San Francisco. When she glided into Woosing harbor with the admiral's two-starred flag flying from her foremast, the American warships assembled there thundered out a fifteen-gun salute in honor of the arriving commanding officer.

Rodgers was well pleased with his assignment. All the officers and men serving in ships of the Asiatic Fleet were volunteers. "I am giving you the cream of the Navy," Robeson had written to Rodgers, "the best ships, men, and armament we have. I know you will use them well and bring only honor to our country and our flag. . . ."

4 "IF WE MAKE NO MOVE..."

AMONG THE FIRST PROBLEMS THAT CONFRONTED Rodgers was the Korean question. A delegation of American traders came to him with a request that the navy provide escort for merchant ships plying the waters off Korea.

They also asked Rodgers to press for a trade agreement with the Hermit Kingdom. The admiral was impressed by the glowing picture they painted of untold riches awaiting American business if only it had access to the Korean market.

"Admiral, if we don't make a treaty, somebody else will," a shipping agent told Rodgers. "Why should we let the Europeans beat us out? We were the ones who opened Japan. Why can't we do the same for Chosen?"

Why not, indeed, Rodgers wondered.

The businessmen had convinced him that the Land of the Morning Calm was a mercantile treasure chest; a trader's Garden of Eden. If Uncle Sam could beat the competition to that opulent marketplace, it would benefit not only American business but the whole nation as well. Rodgers was a firm believer in the maxim "What is good for business, is good for America."

This was the era of commercial expansionism; in post-Civil War America, domestic markets had grown a hundredfold as the country spread westward and rail networks crisscrossed the vast regions of the frontier.

However, this huge domestic market was not enough for American businessmen. They wanted an ever greater share of foreign trade which had increased immeasurably during the last decade. This was especially true in the Orient. As every mercantile power scrambled for bigger markets in China and Japan, Korea loomed more important than ever.

Businessmen were irked by the tightly shut portals

of that country. They were tantalized by the rumors of the tremendous wealth denied them by Seoul's exclusion policies. American traders put forth every effort and inducement to make the Koreans change their ways; but all these overtures were rebuffed.

John Rodgers also wanted the Hermit Kingdom opened to trade—preferably American. He had a personal stake in seeing this achieved. If he played a leading role in winning a commercial treaty for America from Prince Tai-Wun, his place in history would be assured. Along with Commodore Perry, he would be hailed as one of the men who opened the Orient.

Rodgers could not act on his own. He needed orders from his superiors before undertaking any action about Korea. Since he was a good, methodical officer, the admiral proceeded to assemble all the information available on the Hermit Kingdom. One man he consulted was George F. Seward, the United States consul general in China.

Seward was a diplomat with good connections in Washington. Former Secretary of State William Seward was his uncle. However, ability, not nepotism, had obtained for George Seward his post in China. He was one of the few career diplomats at that time who might be considered an expert on the Far East.

A widely traveled man, Seward knew the Orient
and its problems both from on-the-spot studies and
from exhaustive research. He was keenly interested
in Korea and had carried on intensive studies of that
country. He was versed in its traditions, customs,
culture, language, and history. With the help of
Chinese trader friends, Seward had compounded an
accurate chart of Chosen's commercial potentialities.

He was well aware of the high-flown stories about
Korea's purported wealth in gems and gold. But
Seward had facts and figures to submerge these
fanciful claims. He deflated Chosen's importance as
a market and a source of trade. Indeed, Seward saw
no need to waste time, effort, and money in an
attempt to forge a trade pact with Korea.

"There is little in that country to attract business,"
he said. "I've heard all the talk among merchants in
Shanghai, Chefoo, Nagasaki, and Tokyo. But these
gentlemen are spouting poppycock. Chosen is a poor
land where the masses barely eke out an existence
and only the ruling clique enjoys affluence. In my
considered opinion a trade agreement would be of
little material benefit to the United States and might
prove more trouble than it was worth."

Although Seward's bleak view of the Hermit Kingdom as a potential customer for American goods was
in direct contrast to the general opinion, Rodgers

changed his mind and accepted the consul general's outlook.

In a report to Secretary of the Navy Robeson, Admiral Rodgers said: "Mr. Seward speaks with authority backed on solid information. He has shown me irrefutable evidence to prove his points. . . . I no longer believe that our main thrust regarding Chosen should be aimed at a trade treaty . . . but rather an agreement to cover wrecked mariners. . . ."

Seward also strongly advocated some sort of treaty regarding American sailors who might be shipwrecked on the Korean coast. According to the consul general, the chances of working out such an accord were good. Seoul had already made faint overtures by hinting to the Chinese that the government wanted to clarify to the Americans its position on the *General Sherman* affair.

Seward thought the Chinese might be persuaded to act as intermediaries between the United States and Korea on the matter of shipwrecked sailors. In any event, he urged, it was worth a try. "If we make no move to protect our seamen from cruel and barbarous treatment, we have failed in our duty as Americans," Seward declared.

As the ranking United States naval officer in that area, Rodgers felt that one of his most important functions was to assure the safe passage of American ships and their crews. However, before taking any steps toward a concord with the Koreans, the admiral reported to Robeson:

> Even if the Koreans should be adverse to any stipulations regarding shipwrecked sailors, this does not seem to be a reason why our government should not demand their good treatment and safe delivery to the nearest consul in China or in Japan. . . . In Korea, not only may shipwrecked crews be murdered, but unprotected villagers of that country are liable to be robbed and maltreated by our sailors. . . . Therefore it seems proper to secure the rights of having an agent in Korea to handle events . . . relating to our own shipping. This would prepare the way for a more extended treaty, should such . . . prove to be desirable at a later date. . . .

After sending off that dispatch to Washington, Admiral Rodgers settled down to the task of running the Asiatic Station. While there was seldom anything of a spectacular nature for his ships to do, both vessels and men were kept busy.

Occasionally a gunboat patrolling the Yangtze River might have to trade shots with river pirates. Sometimes American bluejackets clashed with the bandits, raiding their river-shore hideouts. But this sort of action was rare. The days, weeks, and months were taken up with mundane chores: scraping, swabbing decks, painting, gun drills, target practice, cleaning weapons, polishing brass, keeping everything shipshape.

Except for the flagship *Colorado*, few of Rodgers' vessels ever remained for an extended stay at the main base in Woosing, or the other bases at Chefoo, Nagasaki, and Yokohama. Gunboats and sloops were usually at sea making hydrographic surveys along the coast, charting rivers, moving from station to station, if for no reason other than to show the American flag in the various treaty ports.

This activity was also designed to keep crews on the alert and to acquaint all hands with every sector under the jurisdiction of the Asiatic Station.

The one region that remained virtually unknown to Americans was the coastline of Chosen. However, very soon, Admiral Rodgers and his staff would be studying the available hydrographic charts of the Hermit Kingdom's west coast, the headwaters of the Han River, and the approaches to Seoul. The men of the Asiatic Fleet, who were growing tired of drab chores, were destined soon to taste more action than any one of them had contemplated facing.

"I WANT MY MEN PREPARED..." 5

FOR A LONG TIME, RODGERS HEARD NOTHING FROM
the Secretary of the Navy. He did not even get an
acknowledgment that his report had been received.
Twice monthly, packet boats arrived at Woosing
carrying mail for the fleet and dispatches from the
State and Navy departments. As the weeks rolled
by, Rodgers admitted to an aide, "I'm convinced
that the Secretary has consigned my report to a trash
basket."

In June 1870, four months after he had submitted

the report, Rodgers had word about it. The comments neither came from Secretary Robeson nor were they addressed to Rodgers. One day, the United States ambassador to China, Frederick F. Low, arrived in Woosing from Shanghai, accompanied by his staff and Consul General Seward. Low brought with him a message of the utmost importance from Secretary of State Hamilton Fish. Robeson had forwarded Rodgers' report to the State Department, believing that it dealt with matters that fell more within Fish's jurisdiction than within his own.

The Secretary of State brought the question of bargaining for a Korean treaty directly to President Ulysses S. Grant. The President decided that such negotiations must be conducted at the top level by the ambassador to China.

Low's instructions from Fish were simple and to the point. The Secretary delegated to the ambassador the authority to "secure from the Korean authorities at Seoul an agreement for the protection of shipwrecked American mariners . . . and, if possible, a satisfactory pact regulating trade between the United States and Chosen. . . ."

The State Department also noted that as Commander in Chief, Asiatic Fleet, Rear Admiral Rodgers was to accompany Low "with a display of force adequate to support the dignity of the United States government."

Attached to Fish's message were copies of the Treaty of Yedo and the Treaty of Kanagawa which Commodore Perry had negotiated with Japan. Low was to guide himself by the contents of these two documents. In a footnote, Rodgers was ordered to accommodate the ambassador and his party aboard the *Colorado*. Ambassador Low was considered to be in charge of the expedition "in all matters pertaining to policy and of a political nature." He was outranked by Rodgers only on strictly naval questions.

The operation, named the Korean Treaty Expedition, was scheduled to start in May 1871, an interval of almost eleven months. The reason for this delay concerned weather conditions. May brought the mildest and most constant weather to that region. Also, Rodgers required time to collect hydrographic and navigational data on the western coast of Korea.

In addition, the admiral had to reassemble the various units of his fleet that were off on missions to the farthest corners of the Asiatic Station. Then, too, it would take months to equip the fleet with sea stores, rations, medical supplies, ordnance, and all the items needed for a sizable naval expedition in foreign, possibly hostile waters.

Ambassador Low was amenable to that long hiatus so that he might explore the possibilities of attaining an agreement with Seoul through the Chinese. If this could be worked out, it would not be necessary to carry out the Korean Treaty Expedition, thus saving the United States both money and bother.

Despite every diplomatic maneuver, Low could make little headway with the Chinese, who seemed reluctant to get involved in this affair. A few years earlier a new element had been injected into the relationships that China had with the West. During the late 1860's, political forces with an antiforeign philosophy started gaining ground in China. By 1870 they had made deep inroads, and officials who had formerly cooperated with Europeans and Americans now became difficult to deal with.

Regulations and procedures were changed almost daily. Every possible trick was used to harass foreigners. According to Low: "It was a time of frustration for us. . . . The Chinese dallied and delayed until it seemed impossible to maintain one's temper and diplomatic aplomb. . . . Important and urgent messages went astray or were pigeonholed and never acted upon. . . . The Chinese, in my opinion, were resorting to subtle sabotage. . . . While they listened politely and respectfully to official complaints, nothing ever was done to rectify the situation. . . ."

After much prodding and many weeks of delay, the Chinese finally forwarded a letter from Low to Prince Tai-Wun in Seoul. Low was to write later, "I knew not whether the Prince had actually received my communication in which I expressed our desire to obtain a 'shipwrecked mariners' arrangement with him. In any event, total silence was the only response from Seoul. . . . After waiting a reasonable period for a reply, I informed Admiral Rodgers that we would proceed with the expedition. . . ."

Preparatory activities intensified during the early months of 1871. Vessels bringing supplies from the United States for the fleet dropped anchor at Woosing. On the days these ships arrived, the seamen of the Asiatic Fleet worked hard hauling stores aboard their own craft.

When not loading stores, the bluejackets went through rigorous training schedules. Landing parties rehearsed storming ashore from small boats. They drilled with bayonet and rifle. Officers of the Colorado's marine detachment ran grueling sessions on infantry tactics for the sailors.

Hour after hour, under a blazing sun, the bluejackets went through arduous infantry training. They learned to take cover, advance by rushes, form skirmish lines, and dig trenches, and spent many days sweltering on the rifle range.

One seaman off the *Colorado* wrote in his diary: "Had I wished to be a soldier, I would have enlisted in the army—not the navy! The officers, especially those accursed leathernecks, seem to have gone quite mad over drilling us. . . ."

Despite the grumbling of his men, Admiral Rodgers watched the progress of the training with satisfaction. Aware that the sailors were displeased, he told an aide, "I can scarcely blame them for complaining. They are not soldiers, but sailors. But should we meet opposition in Korea and be forced to fight on land, I want my men prepared. . . ."

Everything was ready for the expedition by late April 1871. Ships of the Asiatic Fleet were assembled both at Woosing and at Nagasaki. (The *Colorado*, *Palos*, and *Monocacy* rode anchor off Woosing. The *Alaska* and *Benecia* were moored at Nagasaki.)

Ambassador Low and his entourage came to Woosing on April 27. Low brought with him a staff of fifty persons—secretaries, interpreters, aides, and servants. He also brought five Korean sailors who had been shipwrecked and cast ashore on the coast of China. The ambassador reasoned he could create some goodwill by returning these men to their native land.

Low's party was so large that all of them could not be provided for on the *Colorado*. Some of the less important personnel were quartered on the *Palos*, and a few had to be taken aboard the *Monocacy*. Later, they were transferred to the *Alaska* and the *Benecia*, which had more commodious and comfortable accommodations than the gunboats.

There were varied predictions about the outcome of the Korean Treaty Expedition. Low privately admitted that he was pessimistic and did not expect to accomplish much on this mission. He was discouraged by the attitude of the Chinese and by his own ignorance of Korea.

"I find myself less than sanguine of achieving any success. Despite all my efforts I have learned very little of Chosen. . . . Mr. Seward has filled me in with much background, but in my opinion, the Hermit Kingdom is more of a sealed book than Japan was before Commodore Perry's visit there," Low wrote in a letter to a friend in Washington.

On the other hand, Admiral Rodgers seemed cheerful about the mission's prospects. Only a few days before sailing to Korea, he told the officers of the *Colorado:*

Anticipations vary as to the reception we shall probably meet. I will hope, until fact dispels hope, that we shall meet with success. The time has come for the Koreans to make a treaty. If we do not succeed, some other power or powers will be more fortunate. That is why we must not fail. . . .

Although Rodgers kept up a sunny front before his officers and men, he was not quite so buoyant in private. The admiral confided to his journal shortly before sailing:

There is a cloud hanging over this operation. In the first place, we know almost nothing of the Koreans and their ways, except that which Mr. Seward has told us. . . . Now, this lack is bad enough. One should have some idea about the nature of a potential adversary, just as it is of equal import to know the true character of a possible friend. . . . But even more disturbing to me in a technical sense, we have been unable to ascertain many facts about the waters and the coast of western Korea. . . . We have only the charts drawn up by the Frenchman Admiral Rozé, five years ago, when he led his ill-starred expedition to the Hermit Kingdom. . . ."

"I PREDICT THAT ALL WILL GO SMOOTHLY..." 6

IF RODGERS HARBORED SOME SECRET DOUBTS AND forebodings about the venture, so did the marines and sailors who manned the ships. The scuttlebutt (naval slang for gossip) in the fo'c'sles where the crewmen were quartered was colored by vivid rumors about Korea and its people. All the old stories were rehashed and salted with fresher, wilder fantasies.

Somehow the rumor spread that the Koreans were armed with a secret weapon which could blow apart even an ironclad warship, so great and powerful was the explosive device it hurled. Another described in gruesome detail the tortures Koreans used on prisoners. Although these blood-curdling facts were entirely imaginary, they quickly made the rounds of the fleet. Soon every man in the squadron was ready to take an oath that he had been told the story firsthand from a "survivor" or at least from an "eyewitness."

According to the scuttlebutt which was attested to by men who had never been there, Chosen was overrun with "wild beasts," "cavemen," "savage females," "rivers of boiling hot water," and "deadly snakes."

As the rumors grew and flourished, one perceptive young sailor wrote home:

> This stupid talk is endless. There's no use trying to be logical and showing that this scuttlebutt is arrant nonsense. The men don't want to hear logic. They prefer fantasy and dwell on it hour after hour. . . . Somehow, such gossip helps ease their fears of the unknown into which we soon will be heading. . . . In my opinion, only the stupidest and dullest of our men take any stock in these foolish yarns. . . .

Perhaps, as the sailor believed, the crewmen were able to mask their own fears in the purple fantasies they spun. No doubt they were performing an age-old ritual conducted by fighting men since the first warriors locked in combat. A man prepared himself for battle by imagining the worst and talking about it. His fancy always portrayed the foe as fiercer, stronger, and better armed than he actually was. The dangers that lay ahead were enlarged and exaggerated. Once a man aired these secret terrors, he was ready to cope with the real ones as they confronted him.

When it became quite apparent to the men that the sailing date was close at hand, the awesome rumors stopped. Many sailors and marines in the Asiatic Fleet were Civil War veterans who had been under fire in that conflict. Once action was in the offing, they no longer wasted energy in idle talk, but pitched into their duties more vigorously than ever. The old-timers set an example for the recruits, and the ships were made ready for departure without delay.

Ambassador Low and the leading members of his staff were piped aboard the *Colorado* on April 28, 1871. The remainder of his entourage was welcomed on the *Palos* and the *Monocacy*.

At noon, Admiral Rodgers' two-starred flag was raised to the *Colorado*'s foremast. Signal pennons spelling out the command "All Ships Sortie! Follow Me!" went fluttering up a halyard. The frigate nosed out into the slipstream, followed by the *Monocacy* and the *Palos*. On shore, a small crowd of spectators cheered, while a navy band played martial airs.

The three ships made an uneventful run to Nagasaki where the *Alaska* and the *Benecia* awaited them. Clearing up last-minute details, loading additional stores, and a spell of unusually foul weather occupied almost two weeks' time. However, on Tuesday, May 6, everything was in readiness. Early that morning, in sparkling sunshine, the squadron steamed out of Nagasaki harbor bound for the Land of the Morning Calm.

The five ships sailed in formation with the *Colorado* leading, followed by the *Alaska* and the *Benecia* abreast. The *Monocacy* brought up the rear, while the *Palos,* acting as a tender for the flagship, held her station off the port beam of the *Colorado.*

For the first time since Commodore Perry's voyage of 1853, units of the American Navy were heading to a foreign shore for the purpose of obtaining a treaty. Actually, this mission differed from Perry's. On his trip to Japan, Commodore Perry had been given full powers by President Millard Fillmore to negotiate with the Japanese. Rodgers, however, lacked the authority that had been delegated to Perry. All questions relating to a possible treaty with the Koreans would be dealt with by Ambassador Low. State Department, jealous of its prerogatives, had insisted that this time a diplomat, not a naval officer, was to negotiate the treaty.

After all his years in the service, Rodgers knew how to keep off the shoals of intradepartmental strife. His assignment was to ferry Low to Chosen and bring him safely back. Perhaps he secretly longed to round out his career with a diplomatic coup to equal Perry's, but if so, he gave no outward sign of it, nor did he display even a trace of disappointment.

From the outset, Rodgers was courteous and efficient. Although the presence of Low and the diplomatic staff taxed the facilities of the *Colorado* and caused some crowding, the relations between the ambassador and the crew were extremely cordial.

For the first two days out of Nagasaki, the good weather held. Captain George Cooper of the *Colorado* plotted a course for Korea that had been set out in the charts prepared for Admiral Rozé by French hydrographers. The first American landfall was a group of small islands off the Korean coast known on Rozé's maps as the Ferrières. (The islands were so named in honor of the French town Ferrières, near Paris, where Admiral Rozé had been born.) The five American ships made this point their initial stopping place, reaching there on May 19 in worsening weather.

The area was closed in by a thick, pea-soup fog; the gray curtain held for five days while the ships rode at anchor, nearly hidden from view at a distance of less than fifty yards. The men fretted over the delay. The damp mist swirling about played on nerves. Tempers flared. Bitter arguments erupted in fo'c'sles, and fistfights broke out.

Up on the quarterdeck, the officers masked growing irritation as day after day passed without sunshine and no sign that the impenetrable fog blanket would lift. Admiral Rodgers paced the chart room of the *Colorado* puffing furiously on one cigar after another.

Years later, one of his aides remembered: "The admiral strode back and forth, back and forth, like a caged bear. About his head hung dense clouds of cigar smoke. Between the fog and his cigars, the air in the chart room grew fetid. From time to time the admiral would growl, 'Oh, this damned fog! It's smothering us! You can't even breathe in here!' He did not seem to realize that his cigars, not the fog, were responsible for the smothering. . . ."

So it went. Rodgers fussed and fumed about the bad weather. Ambassador Low did not even appear on deck or in the chart room. He remained sulking in his cabin. An aura of gloom enveloped the entire expedition.

The fog persisted until May 24, when it vanished as suddenly as it had come. The crews greeted the sunshine with rousing cheers. Everyone's spirits rose, and all traces of ill humor were dispelled with the fog. No sooner had the mists cleared than the *Colorado* again signaled, "Follow Me," and the flotilla left the Ferrières. The ships sailed to a body of water on the west coast of Chosen designated on the French charts as Rozé Roads. There the group halted once more.

The ships' steam launches, carrying 12-pounders in their bows and manned by landing parties armed with rifles and sidearms, were lowered. Moving in single file, the launches headed up a channel that led to an excellent anchorage site near the mouth of the Han River. Proceeding slowly, taking soundings as they went, the steam launches carefully explored the channel.

Their findings showed that it was navigable from Rozé Roads to the anchorage for ships of larger size than the *Colorado*. The reconnaissance lasted four days, and during that time, the launch crews saw local people watching from the tree-lined shore. But during the first day or two, all attempts to make contact with the locals failed; the onlookers fled when the boats headed toward them.

On the third morning, a junk intercepted a steam

launch. One of the men on the Korean craft tossed a rock with a note wrapped around it aboard the launch. The junk then shot back to shore.

The note, which was written in Chinese, was brought to Ambassador Low on the *Colorado*. Translated, the missive proved to be from the prefect, or province governor. He asked the nationality and purpose of the visitors, but stated that at the present time he would not have a personal meeting with them. Any answer to his letter was to be attached to a stake and placed on a certain small island in mid-channel.

Ambassador Low prepared a reply, explaining to the prefect why the Americans had come to Chosen. The ambassador requested that his note be forwarded to Prince Tai-Wun. Following instructions, the Americans affixed Low's letter to a stake and put it on the designated island. The next day, the message was gone.

Meanwhile, the launch party returned to Rozé Roads with a full report delivered to Admiral Rodgers by Lieutenant Commander Henry Picking, who had commanded the reconnaissance. Rodgers welcomed the news that the channel was navigable. Without further delay, the squadron sailed on to the anchorage that was noted on Rozé's map as Boisée Anchorage. The site was a short distance upstream from the mouth of the Han and only a few miles downriver from Kanghwa Island.

Rodgers and Low decided that their best strategy was to wait at Boisée Anchorage until the Koreans made some move. They were hopeful that Low's note would be sent to the Prince and receive a favorable reception from him.

The Americans did not have long to wait. On May 30, the day after the ships had arrived at Boisée Anchorage, a large junk approached the *Colorado*. The province prefect, wearing handsome ceremonial robes, was in the craft accompanied by several district officials. The Koreans indicated that they wanted to confer with the foreigners.

A Jacob's ladder was lowered and the Koreans clambered aboard the frigate. After the customary amenities had been observed—introductions, bowing, handshaking—the prefect said that Prince Tai-Wun had received Low's message and was selecting a delegation to meet with the Americans. The reason for the prefect's visit was to set up an appointment.

Low could barely conceal his pleasure when this was translated. He arranged to meet the Seoul delegates the next day at 10 A.M. aboard the *Colorado*. This arrangement was satisfactory to the prefect who then departed with his followers.

After the Koreans had gone, Low grinned at

Rodgers. "Admiral," he said, "I've had a complete change of heart. As you know, I've been pessimistic about this mission from the beginning. But now I believe it's going to be a lot easier than I had imagined. I predict that all will go smoothly from now on."

"DON'T FIRE UNLESS FIRED UPON!" 7

UNHAPPILY FOR THE AMERICANS, AMBASSADOR LOW turned out to be a poor prophet. The visit of the Korean delegates from Seoul brought great disappointment. The men chosen by Prince Tai-Wun arrived promptly at the appointed time, but they were low-ranking officials whom Low characterized as "little more than messenger boys."

Under questioning, the Koreans admitted that they had neither the authority nor instructions to conduct negotiations of any sort. They had been sent

71

by the Prince to demand that the Americans leave at once; they were not welcome in Chosen.

Ambassador Low told the Koreans that the Americans were not leaving; they intended to remain until Prince Tai-Wun was willing to negotiate a treaty in good faith. The ambassador further stated that on June 1, the next day, American survey parties were going upriver to reconnoiter the river beyond Kanghwa and up to the approaches to Seoul. He requested that these parties be permitted to go about their mission unmolested and in peace. He was assured that the surveyors would not be harmed.

After a round of bowing and handshaking, the delegation left the *Colorado*. When they were off the ship, Low admitted to Rodgers that he again was quite concerned and worried. In another turnabout, the ambassador glumly remarked, "The Koreans are stalling, Admiral. They have something up their sleeves, and I don't think we'll like what they produce."

A sharp lookout was kept on all ships during the night, but the Koreans made no move.

The next day, June 1, at 12 noon, four steam launches, trailed by the *Palos* and the *Monocacy*, left the squadron and steamed upriver on the first leg of the survey mission. The expedition, which consisted of 220 men armed with cutlasses, pistols, and rifles, was under the joint leadership of Commander Homer Blake of the *Alaska* and Lieutenant Commander Edward McCrea of the *Monocacy*.

The leading launch, which came off the *Benecia*, was equipped with a 25-pounder in her bow. The three others had 12-pounders. Just before they took off, Admiral Rodgers signaled: "Don't fire unless fired upon! But if you are, don't be the first to stop firing! Good luck!"

Crewmen lined the ships' railings as the launches and gunboats churned away. The sailors cheered and waved; the bluejackets in the launches shouted back until they sailed out of sight around a river bend. Those remaining behind resumed their duties. They could do nothing now but hope and wait for the safe return of the launches, the gunboats, and all who served in them.

Almost from the outset, the surveying party ran into difficulties. The river was at flood tide, and the current raced so swiftly that the launches and two gunboats proved quite unmanageable at the slow speed required for sounding and surveying. Trying to handle the craft, making headway against the rapid current, and taking soundings all at the same time kept the crews on the jump. The launches, especially, had trouble bucking the stream. After traveling less than a mile, the propeller of the *Benecia's* launch became fouled in floating debris and the craft was forced to pull in to shore in order to free the blades. This mishap temporarily removed the 25-pounder from any possible action as the rest of the launches and the gunboats swept past the disabled launch and soon hove into sight of Kanghwa Island.

Kanghwa sat in the river like a monstrous whale; its hills rose in humpbacked crests, looming blue and purple in the distance. The lookout on the launch *Weehawken* (named for the ship that Admiral Rodgers had commanded in the Civil War), which had taken over the lead position, spotted troops moving about on the island where redstone forts and redoubts lined the shore.

Scores of soldiers were seen on parapets and ramparts. A *Weehawken* crewman recalled later that the Koreans were clad in uniforms which consisted of a white coat and white "pajama-type" trousers that were "bound at the ankle." The soldiers wore "conical-shaped" straw hats and a type of sandal commonly seen in Japan and China. According to the observer, the Koreans seemed "less soldierly" in appearance than any other troops he had ever seen.

Brightly colored flags and banners fluttered from the walls and battlements of the forts. A huge standard, on the flagstaff of what seemed to be the main fortress or citadel, was inscribed with Chinese characters and indicated the presence of a prominent general. It was clear to Blake and McCrea that the Koreans must have rushed troops down from Seoul to man the forts, for earlier reconnaissances had shown the bastions to be deserted as late as the previous day.

About this time, a second accident occurred. The *Monocacy* swung too close inshore and rammed against rocks, opening a seam and taking on water. McCrea signaled the *Palos* that he was dropping back to inspect the damage.

The launches, led by the *Weehawken*, veered to port, to pass around Kanghwa on that side. As the column of American vessels filed past the forts at a range of about eight hundred yards, with the *Palos* coming close up in the rear, a battery opened up on the gunboat. This initial salvo was followed by a furious bombardment from the forts and other shore batteries. Although bracketed, the *Palos* and the launches were not hit by shells.

Commander Blake raised the signal "All Ships! Fire at Will!" The Americans responded vigorously to the forts. Within minutes the naval craft had scored on the batteries and the redoubts. Explosions ashore, followed by dancing flames and thick smoke, indicated that at least one magazine had been hit.

At the first gunfire, Master Seaman Seaton Schroder, commanding the *Benecia's* launch, was supervising the clearing of his propellers. When he heard the shooting, Schroder grabbed an ax and with powerful strokes slashed the debris that had ensnarled the blades.

Minutes later, the launch was heading upriver at flank speed, her 25-pounder cleared for action and loaded. The sound of guns also reached the *Monocacy*, which had anchored close to shore while her engineers were patching the leaking seam.

As the guns continued to boom, Lieutenant Commander McCrea ordered his vessel to be put under way. "I don't care if we ship enough water to set the decks awash," he cried. "There's a fight up ahead and we're not going to miss it!"

With water sloshing in her hold, the *Monocacy* waddled clumsily along, only to be passed by the launch which roared by tossing up bow waves and leaving a frothing trail of wake. By the time Schroder's launch reached the battle zone, the rest of the flotilla had run the gantlet of Kanghwa's guns and rounded the island. Out of range and sight of the foe, the Americans regrouped.

The forts opened fire again when the *Benecia's* launch came into view, with the *Monocacy* lurching some distance behind. The smaller craft sped

through a blizzard of shot and shell, her own 25-pounder belching away at the land batteries. A crewman remembered that every time the howitzer went off, "the blast shook our launch from stem to stern. The recoil nearly tore us apart, but Schroder kept yelling, 'Hit 'em again! Hit 'em again!' so we continued to fire the big gun until we rounded the point and rejoined the other ships. . . ."

Some time later, the *Monocacy* ran that same passage. "The only reason we weren't blown out of the water was the incredibly poor marksmanship of the Korean gunners. They were so bad as to be ludicrous," Lieutenant Commander McCrea recalled.

Once the flotilla was reunited, Commander Blake and Lieutenant Commander McCrea had to make a decision. According to their orders from Admiral Rodgers, the surveying party was supposed to push upriver all the way to Seoul. But when they took stock, the officers realized that this could not be accomplished.

McCrea reported that while the *Monocacy*'s leaks had been plugged, his gunboat was still taking on water. The launches signaled that ammunition for their guns was almost expended. The *Palos* had suffered superficial damage from the blast and recoil of her own broadsides. It was clear that the only sensible course was to sail back to Boisée Anchorage.

In addition, two men on the *Alaska's* launch had been wounded by shell fragments and needed treatment.

The *Palos* signaled the others to turn about for the trip downriver. With the *Benecia's* launch leading the way and the two gunboats guarding the rear, the column made the homeward run, aided by the swirling current. As they rounded the island, the Americans braced for the anticipated racketing of enemy guns. But the forts were silent and the flotilla sped past without a shot fired at them.

"The Koreans apparently had taken enough punishment for the present," an officer of the *Palos* jotted in his diary. "They had no stomach for any more that day."

The early return of the surveying party put a damper on American morale. After hearing reports from Blake and McCrea, Ambassador Low was especially upset and worried. "The expedition has received a severe check," the ambassador said. "I don't know what yet will transpire, but I think this shooting has dashed all hope of us gaining our ends peaceably."

Both Rodgers and Low agreed that something had to be done about the Koreans firing on American ships. It was a prime insult to the flag and could not go unpunished. After some discussion, the expedition's leaders decided that punitive action must be taken against the forts. "If we fail to do so," Low declared, "our prestige in the Orient will suffer a serious setback. This affront to the Stars and Stripes must be countered with the sternest measures."

Rodgers agreed with him wholeheartedly. Indeed, he was ready to mount an attack the following morning, June 2. However, when it actually came down to initiating a shooting confrontation, Low had second thoughts. He persuaded Rodgers to delay until June 10, before resorting to force.

"A hiatus of eight or nine days will give Seoul a breathing spell—time to apologize for the hostile action taken against us," Low reasoned. "It might also prove advantageous to our mission of obtaining a treaty. We must bear in mind always that we are here for peaceful purposes, not to wage war."

Admiral Rodgers gave his somewhat reluctant approval to a delay; he was of the "strike-while-the-iron-is-hot" school and felt that the Koreans should be chastised at once. However, he later admitted that his original plan to attack on June 2 had been ill-conceived.

"I was too impulsive in my reaction," the admiral stated. "In the heat of the moment, I overlooked the intricacies of mounting a punitive expedition. I do not doubt that Ambassador Low saved me from a costly blunder. I might have rushed headlong into an operation without making ample provisions for its success. Unquestionably, this was the cause of the French disaster in 1866."

The waiting period allowed the Americans time to perfect their plans for punishing the Koreans. It also enabled the flotilla's mechanics to properly repair the *Monocacy* and the *Palos*. The days were spent in mobilizing and equipping forces to carry out the forthcoming showdown with the Koreans.

"WE WANT NOTHING OF YOURS" 8

ADMIRAL RODGERS DREW UP AN ORDER OF BATTLE which was uncomplicated and straightforward. He intended to put a strong landing force on Kanghwa Island under cover of a heavy naval bombardment; once ashore, the force of marines and sailors would demolish the works on the island.

Since the survey party had been unable to complete its task, Rodgers had insufficient information about the river and dared not risk sending the *Colorado*, the *Benecia*, or the *Alaska* into uncharted waters upstream. The burden of supporting the landing would be upon the *Monocacy* and the *Palos,* since both these shallow draft vessels had already sailed in the Kanghwa area.

In addition to demolishing the Korean works, the landing force was to "spike guns, blow up arsenals, magazines, and ammunition dumps. . . ." Looting, destruction of personal or private property, or any nonmilitary buildings would be severely dealt with, Rodgers warned.

In a general order to his men, the admiral stressed:

> We are Americans engaged in a punitive operation against a people who have insulted our flag. . . . This was the work of a handful of military satraps and their minions. . . . It is upon them that our blows must fall, not the civil populace. . . . Great care and every precaution must be taken to avoid harming any and all civilians and civilian property. . . . Remember that we are not vindictive, but will allow no one to sully American honor with impunity. . . . Conduct yourselves courageously and gallantly in the best traditions of the naval service—as I know you will!"

The landing force would be mustered from men of the *Colorado, Benecia,* and *Alaska;* these ships had the largest crews and could provide a total of 542 sailors and 109 marines to storm Kanghwa Island. An additional group of 128 sailors would man the support vessels, steam launches, and longboats that were to carry the landing force.

Commander Homer Blake of the *Alaska* was selected to be in charge of the overall operation. The skipper of the *Benecia,* Commander Lewis Kimberley, was to lead the landing force. Kimberley's executive officer on the *Benecia,* Lieutenant Commander Winfield Scott Schley, would serve as adjutant to the landing force.

The 109 marines drawn from the detachments on the *Benecia,* the *Colorado,* and the *Alaska* were commanded by Captain Maclane Tilton. With the inclusion of the leathernecks as shock troops for the landing force, Admiral Rodgers' disposition of the attack units was complete.

Preparations for the operation stirred up a busy time aboard all the American ships in Boisée Anchorage. Cooks worked furiously preparing rations. Ammunition was loaded. The men spent long hours cleaning and inspecting weapons. All personal equipment was checked and rechecked.

Once the *Monocacy's* leaking seams had been repaired, her firepower was increased by the addition of two 9-pounders taken from the *Colorado* and remounted on the gunboat. She also carried six 25-pounders, as did the *Palos;* this armament made the two vessels formidable bombardment ships.

While getting his forces ready for the offensive, Rodgers sent out patrols to keep the Korean positions under surveillance. Scouts in small boats spied upon the Kanghwa fortifications from places of concealment along the river. Their reports indicated a worrisome amount of troop movement on the island. It appeared as though thousands of soldiers were being sent to hold Kanghwa. Indeed, so many reinforcements seemed to be piling in that one American scout became suspicious of all that activity.

Hiding himself in a thicket of reeds on the riverbank, he worked his way up to less than one hundred yards of Kanghwa and watched the troops marching into one of the smaller forts. Picking out an officer mounted on a black and white horse, the wary scout watched carefully through his binoculars. After about an hour, another detachment of troops came marching up to the fort. At the head of the column rode the very same officer on the very same horse that the scout had noticed before.

The American then realized what the Koreans were doing. Aware that they were being observed, the wily Koreans wanted the Americans to think that the forts were manned by vast numbers of soldiers.

To accomplish this, they resorted to an old military subterfuge. Troops marched up to a fort, went in, left through a rear exit, and circled around to repeat the deception. This was a trick as ancient as warfare itself. It probably would have worked had not the scout disbelieved what he was supposed to accept on sight.

When a superior officer asked him what had aroused his suspicions, the scout explained, "From where I was stationed, I noticed that all the soldiers I could see were going into the same fort. That struck me as rather odd. The place seemed hardly large enough to hold so many men. So I kept my eyes peeled and had another look until I figured out what was going on."

Some scouts brought back word that many more guns were being emplaced on the walls of the forts. Observers spotted additional cannon daily. The new pieces seemed to be of a heavy caliber, and their presence troubled Rodgers. He could envision the American landing force being shattered by the enemy guns while still approaching the island.

However, his mind was set at rest when two daring scouts, disguised in native garb, sneaked onto Kanghwa Island. They soon discovered that the awesome artillery mounted on the parapets was fake. The cannon were so-called Quaker guns—heavy logs painted black and shaped like cannon. This was another hoary ruse to frighten off a foe without a battle.

The Koreans were far weaker militarily than they

were trying to make themselves appear. But while each side made ready for a possible clash, the Americans and local officials were exchanging notes. These messages satisfied neither the Americans nor the Koreans. There was no question that Rodgers and Low would have called off their punitive attack if an acceptable apology had come from the Koreans. Instead, the notes from the prefect rang with defiance.

On June 3, a letter addressed to the "American Commander" was found attached to a bamboo pole on a little island near Boisée Anchorage.

The message, signed by the prefect, one Li-Kwan, was translated by Edward B. Drew, Ambassador Low's first secretary and chief interpreter. The note stated that it was impossible for Chosen and the Americans to have any sort of friendly relations. Li-Kwan said in part:

> We, the people of Chosen, want nothing to do with you, or the rest of the outside world. We are content as we are. This is our right and our choice. Wherever you have gone, you foreigners have spread misery and unhappiness. . . . If you are here to change our ways or interfere with our customs, go away at once!
>
> Some years ago, we had dealings with your countrymen Shufeldt and Feibiger. They were not wanted and sailed away. Why do you not do the same, Honorable Admiral Rodgers? Or do you desire to suffer the fate we dealt out to the people called the French

whose bones lie buried in our sacred soil? If that is your wish, we shall fulfill it for you. . . . Be wise, accept our warning, and go without spilling blood. . . .

Having read this bellicose missive, Ambassador Low took a diplomatic tack. He instructed Drew to compose a conciliatory response which would be delivered to Li-Kwan by way of the bamboo-pole "post office." Drew penned a soft reply in which he stressed the peaceful motives of the Americans. "We want nothing of yours," Drew wrote. "Our desire is to reach a fair agreement about the treatment of shipwrecked American mariners who might be cast upon your shore. . . . It is our sincere hope that some time in the future, once we have come to terms on this matter, we may work out a means to trade with you. . . . For now, we seek only to prevent a repetition of the tragic *General Sherman* affair. . . ."

Drew also pointed out that the Koreans must "make amends" for the "unprovoked and wanton attack made by your forces upon our boats which were engaged in carrying out a peaceful survey of the river . . . in the vicinity of Kanghwa Island. . . . All we ask is an official apology from your government. . . ."

The letter was placed on the bamboo pole, and several days later, on June 6, a reply appeared. In his response, Li-Kwan observed that it was not within his power to apologize for the shooting at the American "trespassers." He had forwarded Drew's message to the governor of Kanghwa Province, whose remarks were enclosed.

In flowery tones, Chi-Lian, the governor, told Drew that he had spoken to Tai-Wun who flatly refused to have any dealings at all with the Americans.

However, the Prince had given his word that distressed seamen of all nations, not just Americans, would be "helped and not mistreated" and that they would be "repatriated at the earliest moment possible. . . ." Therefore, stated Chi-Lian, the Americans no longer had any reasons "to tarry in Chosen's territorial waters. . . ."

Chi-Lian further stipulated that there would be no apology forthcoming over the firing on the American flag. "It was upon my orders that the forts resorted to the measures that were taken," the governor said. "The commander of the forts was merely doing his duty by repelling trespassers. . . ."

The governor was eager, he assured the Americans, that they should not leave Chosen with hostile feelings. "Appreciating the hardships of your long voyage . . . I am sending on some articles as a trifling assistance to your table," Chi-Lian wrote. "Also consider this to be a gesture of my personal goodwill. . . . Look for my offerings on the ebb tide. . . ."

A few hours later, when the tide turned, a barge came drifting downriver toward the American ships. It carried a strange cargo: three bullocks, fifty chickens, and more than one thousand eggs.

Although the fleet could have made good use of the eggs and meat, Low and Rodgers deemed it unwise for them to accept gifts from the Koreans at this point. Accordingly, Drew wrote another note, refusing the presents and also warning that if no satisfactory regrets were expressed by the Koreans for firing on the American flag, punitive action would be taken. June 10 was the deadline the Americans set for an acceptable response. In the evening, on the flood tide, the barge was floated back upstream.

Tension grew in the American fleet during the next few days as the deadline began running out. By the evening of June 9, no word had come from the Koreans. Scouts reported to Rodgers that the forts were flying battle flags and that Korean troops had dug entrenchments along the shoreline of Kanghwa Island.

Early June 10, the men of the landing force were aroused. Reveille sounded at 3 A.M.; an hour later, the attack group was served a hearty breakfast of steak, eggs, and coffee. By 5 A.M. the sailors and marines were deployed by platoons and sections into twenty-two longboats, strung together, and attached by stout towlines to the stern of the *Palos.*

In the dim morning light, the invasion fleet jockeyed for position. Up front were the *Colorado's* two steam launches; one of them, the *Weehawken,* carried Lieutenant Commander Henry Picking, who was in charge of the waterborne part of the expedition known as Operation Punishment.

Next in line after the launches came the *Monocacy* with her batteries of 9-pounders and 25-pounders. The *Palos,* with Commander Homer Blake aboard, followed the *Monocacy,* towing the twenty-two longboats filled with 651 bluejackets and leathernecks of the landing force. The launches from the *Alaska* and the *Benecia* brought up the rear. They were to render all assistance and pick up survivors in the event that any of the longboats were hit.

By sunrise Saturday, June 10, 1871, the turbulent and fast-running currents of the Han River changed to a gentler, smoother tide. The American craft bobbed easily on the calm Han River as the sun moved higher, bringing the promise of a bright, hot day.

The sailors and marines sat patiently in the longboats, gripping their rifles and squinting out across the glistening water. They made no jokes, sang no songs, talked very little; most of the men remained silent, wrapped in quiet, personal thoughts.

Aboard the *Colorado*, Admiral Rodgers and Ambassador Low paced the quarterdeck, hoping that a last-minute note might arrive from the Koreans. Even at this late hour it was still possible to cancel Operation Punishment. Both men were reluctant to loose violence. But by 10 A.M., when there was no sign from the Koreans, Rodgers peered at his gold pocket watch, cleared his throat, and said, "Ten o'clock, Mr. Low. We cannot wait any longer. Shall I order the advance to get under way?"

Ambassador Low shrugged. "I have no real desire for this, Admiral. My heart isn't in it, but we must do what has to be done. Give the word, Admiral!"

Rodgers nodded to Captain George Cooper, the skipper of the *Colorado*. "Captain, raise the signal!" he said.

At a word from Cooper a signalman hoisted a string of colored code flags to the foremast top where they flapped in the light breeze. The signal read, "All units move out! Good luck!"

On the *Palos*, Commander Blake eyed the flags for a moment and then barked an order. Two signal rockets arched up from the bow of the gunboat. The whistle of the steam launch *Weehawken* emitted three shrill blasts, and the American armada swung upriver in a long line. The sailors left behind on the flagship and the two sloops sounded a parting cheer to which the men of the landing force responded with a will.

A junior officer on the *Colorado* wrote in his diary: "The sunlight danced on the river making it sparkle like ten thousand diamond tiaras. . . . I watched our boats set sail and could not help but think that it was a shame to start a war on such a splendid day. . . ."

LET THE FOREIGN DOGS COME!

9

THE FORTIFICATIONS ON KANGHWA ISLAND LOOKED impressive and impregnable when seen from the river. They consisted of four stone forts, a number of redoubts, and the great citadel fortress perched atop a hill. Built of redstone, the thick-walled strongholds were sited to cover all the upriver approaches with their cannon. To the front of the forts, down by the river's edge, trenches had been dug and earthen breastworks thrown up.

Shortly after daybreak June 10, there was a great

bustle in and around the forts. Drums rolled, trumpets blared, soldiers marched. From a battlement of the citadel, General Wo-Pei, commander of the Kanghwa forts, directed the defensive moves that were being made.

The general's uniform tunic was adorned with beribboned medals which clanked and clashed when he moved. A short, burly man with a mandarin moustache, he stood spraddle-legged, one hand gripping the jeweled hilt of the curved sword that hung in its sheath at his right side. The general was flanked by a half-dozen aides, all of them bedecked with medals.

General Wo-Pei was one of the country's great military heroes. It was he who had crushed the French invasion of Kanghwa Island; he was now prepared to do the same to the Americans. Looking down at the activity below, the general was pleased with his troops. By Western standards they were miserably equipped and trained, but in the eyes of Wo-Pei, the soldiers appeared to be trim, canny warriors.

The white-uniformed Koreans were armed with ancient muskets of a type known as jingals which, long before, should have been relegated to a museum. The working cannon of the forts—not including the useless Quaker guns—were obsolete relics.

General Wo-Pei's army of more than five thousand men was ludicrous to Western observers. It was not an army at all; these little men in their conical straw hats and white "pajama" suits were not warriors, but paper tigers.

In addition to the jingals, the Koreans had pikes, spears, and swords, a motley collection of weapons which gave the troops an anachronistic appearance; they belonged to the Middle Ages, not to the nineteenth century.

However, neither Wo-Pei, his officers, nor the soldiers saw themselves as anything less than soldiers in a mighty conquering army. Because they had beaten an ineptly led French force, the Koreans had delusions of invincibility. More rational men would have realized the hopelessness of attempting to fight the Americans. Wo-Pei had seen them in action when he fired on the surveying party. They had big guns and aimed them with deadly accuracy. It was suicidal to stand against them.

But the proud Koreans refused to face the unvarnished facts. They were a people steeped in ancient traditions and stubbornly defended that heritage at all costs. The strength of the Americans did not overawe them. Had not the men of Chosen defeated the Japanese in the olden days? Had not the French met disaster on this very island? Had not General Wo-Pei led his heroic soldiers to that glorious victory?

The American trespassers in the garden of Chosen would be meted out the same doom that had befallen the French. The forts of Kanghwa were ready.

Now, as the morning slipped by, the Koreans waited in their trenches and on the walls of the forts, cannon loaded and primed. General Wo-Pei was well satisfied.

Let the foreign dogs come!

He would bury them here on Kanghwa Island.

"PROCEED WITH THE ATTACK!"   10

THE AMERICAN SQUADRON HAD GONE LITTLE MORE
than a mile from Boisée Anchorage when a junk appeared on the river and cut in front of the flotilla.
A man in the bow of the junk was waving a huge
white flag; still another truce flag flew from the mast.

On the *Palos*, Commander Blake felt a surge of
elation. "I thought they might be bringing an elev-
enth-hour communication from Seoul, an apology
that would satisfy Admiral Rodgers and Mr. Low,
thus enabling us to cancel the operation," he later

wrote. "I was overjoyed at the prospect of settling the matter without resorting to bloodshed."

A Korean in a small boat pulled alongside the *Palos,* handed up a sealed envelope, and rowed back to the junk which then headed upriver. Mr. Drew, who was accompanying Operation Punishment as its official interpreter, translated the letter for the commander.

Instead of containing an apology, it was bellicose in tone. Signed by Chi-Lian, the message baldly warned the Americans that the forts on Kanghwa were ready for them. It declared that any further move by the Americans would be regarded as an act of war. "If you do not now turn back," Chi-Lian had written, "you will suffer the consequences of your rashness. Expect no mercy from us. Prisoners taken will be regarded as trespassers and shown no quarter. Leave now or be destroyed!"

When Drew read this to him, Commander Blake grimaced. "I suppose there's nothing left for us but to get on with it," he sighed.

Once again signal flags flew from the topmast of the *Palos,* spelling out: "Proceed with the attack!" The *Weehawken* and her sister launch came up to Kanghwa Island at 11:30 A.M., and the steam launches veered to starboard and port opening up a path for the *Monocacy,* which swung broadside and took her bombardment station at a distance of some nine hundred yards from shore. Her skipper, Lieutenant Commander Edward McCrea, peered through his binoculars at the forts and said to his gunnery officer, "Mr. Simmons, you may open fire at your convenience."

A few minutes later, the guns of the *Monocacy* started laying in a barrage on the shoreline trenches. Through the smoke of exploding shells, the men on the ships could see Koreans scrambling out of the rifle pits and running for the shelter of the nearest forts.

The *Monocacy* steamed along shooting slowly at selected targets. The smaller guns of the launches joined hers. The biting smell of cordite tainted the air, and gunsmoke hung in cloud layers thick enough to blot out the sun.

Immediately after the *Monocacy*'s initial salvo, the forts opened fire. As before, the shore guns laid down a furious counterbombardment, but it was wholly ineffectual due to the usual poor Korean marksmanship. The missiles from the forts did no damage to the Americans. Most of them fell short because the old cannon lacked sufficient range. Some, which had been aimed too high, exploded harmlessly in the water, and a few near misses doused the men in the boats towed by the *Palos*.

While no American was killed or wounded by the Korean shellfire, exposure to it was a terrifying experience, as one marine later admitted. "We were out there like sitting ducks," he said. "Every time one of the big ones went off close by, my heart came up into my throat. I figured that sooner or later we'd catch one. They couldn't keep missing us forever."

For more than an hour, the *Monocacy* and the launches blasted away at the forts and shore batteries but were unable to silence them. Although the shelling from the Korean artillery was inaccurate, it reached such an intensity that Commander Blake had to alter his original battle plan. He had intended to put the landing force ashore on the beach directly in front of the forts when the naval guns had silenced the shore batteries. But since the Americans could not knock out the enemy guns, Blake decided to find an alternate landing area because he did not want to keep the boats exposed to Korean shells any longer than necessary.

Blake signaled Picking to bring the *Weehawken* alongside and come aboard the *Palos* for a conference. Picking complied, and the commander instructed him to seek out another place suitable for a landing.

The *Weehawken* took off with Picking on a run along the island river line. About a mile to the left of the forts, Picking spotted an open grassy plain which was shielded from the view of the forts by a thickly wooded area. Once ashore in this sector, the Americans could move through the woods and attack the forts on the left flank.

Picking signaled his find to Blake who approved the choice. At his orders, the twenty-two longboats were cast off from the *Palos* and from each other. Deploying into a double rank of eleven boats each, with Captain Tilton's marines in the first line, the boats were propelled shoreward by oarsmen who worked the sweeps. Having freed herself of the small boats, the *Palos* joined the *Monocacy* in the prelanding bombardment.

The gunboats so blanketed the Koreans with shellfire that they could do nothing to impede the landings being carried out beyond the woods on the left.

About fifty yards offshore, the longboats grounded on what seemed to be a sandbar in less than a foot of water. The marines who made up the first wave vaulted from their boats at Captain Tilton's command. The leathernecks had expected to land knee-deep in water and sand. Instead, they found themselves trapped in a bog of soft mud. The marines, weighted down with ammunition, packs, and rifles, sank to their waists in the clinging slime. Splashing, floundering, cursing, they inched toward shore.

Behind them, the bluejackets were caught in the

same predicament. Adding to the ordeal, the sun blazed down out of a cloudless sky, as the Americans tried to extricate themselves from the morass into which they had blundered. To further torment them came swarms of gnats, mosquitoes, and black flies, which settled on faces, lips, necks, biting and sting-ing the beleaguered men.

At last, after what seemed like an endless time, the leathernecks staggered onto hard, sun-baked ground. As one marine recalled that landing: "It was a hellish experience to cross those fifty yards. . . . I feared that if I lost my footing, I'd sink down and be buried under the mud. . . . I remember thinking that it was a stupid way for a marine to die, smothered in a bog. . . ."

Panting, sweating, red-faced, mud-smeared, the leathernecks collapsed on the beach. The men seemed utterly spent by their exertions. But when Captain Tilton bellowed, "On your feet!" and non-coms repeated the order, the leathernecks obeyed.

Tilton waved his revolver. "As skirmishers, ad-vance!" he shouted. "Follow me!" The captain headed for the woods with his men trudging after him, their ranks widely spaced out.

Behind them, sailors were stumbling onto the beach, equally exhausted by the trek through the mud. The sweating bluejackets formed up into pla-

toons, voicing complaints, growling and grumbling. "All right," a chief petty officer snarled. "Quit beefing! If you're unhappy, just send a letter to President Grant and he'll set things right! Now get in line and shut up!"

While the main body of the landing force was assembling on the beach, Tilton's marines cleared the woods and rushed a small fort which the defenders had abandoned during the naval bombardment. The stronghold was a stone redoubt standing atop a rocky slope. The marines promptly dubbed the captured bastion Fort Tilton, in honor of their commander. It had been erected close to the woods and on the edge of the plain.

On the right flank, separated by 150 or 200 yards of open land, rose another, larger redoubt. Then came the rest of the forts, spaced out along a front of approximately one mile. To the rear was the citadel and beyond that loomed the hills. A good dirt road connected the string of forts and led into the hills where the thatched roofs of a peasant village could be discerned.

The leathernecks watched shells from the ships bursting on the forts which were swathed in smoke. The naval guns had not yet put the enemy's batteries out of commission. The Koreans were still shooting, and from where Tilton's men stood, they saw shells splashing around the American gunboats and launches.

Tilton lost no time. He sent patrols out to probe the sector to the front and toward the enemy strongpoints. He also dispatched a runner to the main body, asking for orders. While awaiting word from the rear, Tilton had his men take up defensive positions in the captured bastion to check any enemy counterthrust.

The heat was oppressive. The marines quickly drained their canteens and Tilton told off a detail to locate fresh water. That party soon found a fast-flowing stream in the woods nearby, and the men were allowed to go in small groups to refill their canteens.

When Tilton's patrols returned from their reconnaissance mission, they brought back disturbing reports. Although the road was in good-enough condition to take field artillery, the plain on which the landings had been made was not a stretch of level ground, as it appeared to be when seen from the river.

On the contrary, the area was bisected and broken by gullies, deep ravines, and defiles that had not been visible from the water. This was tortuous and difficult terrain the Americans had selected for their landing. Attacking the forts from that direction was not going to be easy.

The sailors and marines would have to attack over rough ground which would slow down the advance and leave them vulnerable to fire from the forts over a long period. Since the ships could not provide covering fire once the attack got under way, support for the assault depended upon the eight fieldpieces that had been sent along with the landing force.

However, getting those pieces off the boats and bringing them ashore through the bog would be a difficult and tedious job. Hauling them into position for bombarding the forts also promised to be a backbreaking chore.

Lieutenant Douglas Cassell, who was in charge of the artillery, came to the landing area with the eight guns carried aboard four longboats. When the boats scraped on the sandbar, Cassell ordered the guns unloaded and dragged ashore. This turned out to be a nightmarish task. The guns were taken off the boats one at a time. Eighty men hauled on the towropes and pulled the fieldpieces through the soft mud.

The sailors pulled and strained, shouted and cursed. Inch by stubborn inch they moved the guns to shore, one by one. Even officers pitched in, heaving on ropes or putting shoulders to artillery carriage wheels. Somehow, the eight fieldpieces were wrestled to the beach. Ammunition for them was passed up from the boats, hand to hand, along a human chain.

By the time this was completed, the afternoon had almost gone. Commander Kimberley, who had taken over the land forces, sent word by runner for Tilton to move up another half mile or so, dig in, and await the arrival of naval infantry under Lieutenant Commander Silas Casey, the following morning. Two fieldpieces were hand-hauled up to Tilton and sited on the flanks of his sector.

Dusk was falling as the worn-out Americans prepared to spend their first night on Korean soil. Although it had been a hellish day for them, the invaders had not taken a single casualty from enemy action. The day's heat was dispelled with the coming of night. A chill wind rose. Darkness brought a drop in temperature which numbed the men in their wet and muddy clothes.

The guns fell silent, and in the still darkness the Americans heard chanting from the Korean forts, a wailing Oriental melody that could have been either a song of defiance or a song of mourning.

"GO AHEAD AND TAKE THE FORTS!" 11

THE NIGHT PASSED UNEASILY FOR THE AMERICANS; there was little sleep for them. Tense sentries made their rounds with cocked rifles, fingers curled on triggers. Men untried in land warfare shied at shadows. A dozen alarms were raised as nervous sailors fired at rustling leaves, even the cry of a night bird, believing them to be sounds made by skulking infiltrators.

Each time the shots went off, fitful sleepers leaped up, weapons gripped, to repel an attack. They were made even more uncomfortable after midnight when a fine rain began falling.

111

The men had eaten little. Cooking fires were forbidden for fear of attracting snipers. The Americans had to make a meal of hardtack washed down by water. The problem of water became urgent. Despite the detailed preparations for the landing force, someone had blundered, and an insufficient number of casks of fresh water had been put aboard the invasion boats. Perhaps those in charge of supplies thought there would be water on Kanghwa Island.

Although Tilton's marines had found fresh water, the main body of the landing force could locate only a few slow-moving, foul-smelling streams. However, driven by need, the men had filled their canteens with this noxious liquid.

At dawn on Sunday, June 11, a thick ground mist covered Kanghwa Island. Bleary-eyed, unwashed, and hungry, the Americans made a tasteless breakfast of hardtack and water.

While the dejected men were eating their miserable fare, Commander Kimberley received bad news from Blake. The gunboat *Palos* had run aground the previous evening while moving to a new bombardment station. Trapped on submerged rocks, the vessel was finally refloated at high tide. However, she was leaking badly, and Blake was not sure that she could take much part in the mission.

This worried Kimberley, who had been counting

on an hour or two of naval bombardment before starting a general attack. Despite the new guns that had been added to her arsenal, the *Monocacy* lacked the power to reduce the forts. In addition to this worry, Kimberley was concerned about the condition of his men. Still worn out by the strenuous exertions of the previous day, they moved about in the mist like listless ghosts. Many had faces and hands badly swollen from insect bites; those most seriously affected were ordered to stay on the beach when the fighting started.

Back at Boisée Anchorage, Rear Admiral Rodgers was up long before daylight. He had arranged for couriers to bring him the latest reports from the field. Early that Sunday morning a boat came downriver with messages from Blake and Kimberley informing Rodgers that the *Palos* probably would be out of action.

This upset the admiral. He had been harboring misgivings ever since the expedition had sailed the morning before. On the night of June 10, he had admitted to Low, "I'm apprehensive as to the outcome of the operation. The enemy doesn't concern me. Our men can handle him easily enough. But I apprehend serious difficulties in the natural obstacles of rocks, shoal water, and the river currents. Had we proper hydrographic charts, I would be serenely confident of success. This way, one never knows what unhappy accident might befall."

However, Rodgers kept his conposure and returned a message to the commanders, which said in part: "Please be assured that I have complete faith in you. If you feel that the loss of the *Palos* might endanger the operation, you are free to withdraw at your own discretion. . . ."

It was 8 A.M. by the time Rodgers' note reached Kimberley. The sun had burned off the ground mist, and even at this early hour the day was hot. A naval veteran with long service, Commander Lewis Kimberley was not a rash man. He never made a move unless certain that every possibility for both success and failure had been considered.

Before taking another step in the operation, Kimberley called for a council of war with the senior officers of the landing force, including Commander Blake who had come ashore from the damaged *Palos*.

Attending the meeting were Kimberley's adjutant, Lieutenant Commander Winfield Scott Schley; Lieutenant Commander Silas Casey of the landing force's right wing; Lieutenant Commander William K. Wheeler, of the left wing; Lieutenant Commander Douglas Cassell of the artillery and his battery commanders, Lieutenant A. S. Snow and Lieutenant W. W. Mead. Captain Tilton of the marines was summoned from his advanced outpost for the conference.

After brief discussion, the officers were unanimous in agreeing to press the attack despite the lack of the *Palos*. According to Commander Blake, that vessel would definitely be unable to lend any assistance.

Speaking as the leader of the entire expedition, Blake told his officers:

Gentlemen, should this mission fall short of success, I want it clearly understood by all present that the sole responsibility of the failure will be mine alone. I am in overall command, and blame for failure is the burden of leadership. The decision of whether or not this attack will be pressed further is mine alone to make. You are here to serve in an advisory capacity only. If we are successful in our endeavor, the praise must be shared by all. If we fail, the censure is solely mine. . . .

Having delivered his statement, Blake turned to Kimberley and said, "Go ahead and take the forts! I'm moving my command post to the *Monocacy* where you can reach me by semaphore. Good luck to you all, gentlemen!"

A few minutes later, Blake was being rowed out to the *Monocacy*. After his departure, Kimberley said to the officers, "Return to your units. There'll be hot work, today! Good luck!"

Soon, whistles were blowing and orders shouted. The men of the landing force slung packs, checked their weapons, adjusted gear. The sailors-turned-infantry formed up in platoons.

From the river, the *Monocacy* started a slow, steady bombardment. At 10:45 A.M. both wings of the landing force began moving toward the forts. The rough ground soon broke up the American formation; deep ditches and ravines separated platoons.

The fieldpieces that were supposed to roll along with the march fell far behind. It was almost impossible for the crews to drag the guns over that lacerated terrain.

The heat became intolerable before long. Some men, especially in the left wing, where the ground was rougher than elsewhere, collapsed with sunstroke and had to be removed from the field on stretchers.

A hospital tent had been pitched, and the casualties were to be given first aid there before being ferried downriver by steam launch to the sick bays of the larger ships. The place selected for the hospital tent was a poor choice. When the first sunstroke victims were brought in, they had to be lugged across the marshy bog to the waiting steam launch after receiving initial treatment. The physical work of carrying the stretchers through the morass in the now unbearable heat was a murderous chore.

One youth, assigned to a stretcher unit, later wrote to his father:

> You who fought at Antietam and Gettysburg will know much about the workings of the military mind. . . . There was stupidity in your day . . . but I doubt whether you came up against the crassness of the officer who decided where that field hospital tent should be raised. . . . I cannot begin to chronicle the agonies we endured hauling those poor lads from the tent to the river through fifty yards of waist-deep mud. . . .

12 "GO GET 'EM!"

THE AMERICANS HAD CROSSED THE PLAIN BY MIDDAY.
On the left, Lieutenant W. W. Mead managed to
bring up two of his four fieldpieces, while the other
two were still being hand-hauled over the scarred
ground. Also on the left, Wheeler's sailor-soldiers regrouped to attack several small redoubts which
blocked their advance to the main citadel known on
the French maps of Kanghwa as Fort du Coude.

Wheeler was waiting for his other two artillery
guns to come up before mounting the assault when a

big force of Koreans suddenly appeared on a ridge about five hundred yards away. The enemy force was positioned to the front of the American lines. Moments after those troops had been spotted, many more Koreans were observed on another ridge to the right of the Americans.

Trumpets shrilled on the ridges, and a great shout went up from the Koreans who swarmed off the high ground and charged at the Americans, the two enemy groups merging into one huge mass.

Without awaiting orders the sailors opened fire at the onrushing foe, but the rifles had little effect against the surging human mass sweeping down on Wheeler's men.

Closer and closer came the foe. Sunlight glinted on waving swords and twinkled off spear tips. As they ran, the Koreans gave out high-pitched cries and their trumpets never stopped blaring.

The order "Fix Bayonets!" rang out in the American lines. Blades clattered and clicked as they were attached to rifles. Involuntarily, the bluejackets drew more closely together. Standing, crouching, and kneeling, almost shoulder to shoulder, they formed a solid rank and braced to meet the onslaught.

The men were so intently watching the approaching enemy that no one noticed Lieutenant Mead's gun crews frantically rolling the two fieldpieces into firing position. Nor did they see the other two guns of the left-wing battery also being brought to bear on the Koreans. Ammunition carriers lugging boxes of shells piled the missiles alongside the guns.

Only about a hundred yards separated the front ranks of the enemy from the Americans, and the gap was closing fast. As one sailor recalled: "There must have been three or four thousand of them heading straight for us. . . . I thought it might well be my last hours upon this earth. . . . I fired my rifle again and again, grateful that it was a repeater and not a single-shot musket, but no matter how much we fired, the enemy still pressed on. . . ."

Some of the Koreans were armed with antiquated jingals and stopped to shoot at the Americans. Those antiquated muskets made a fearful noise, but they could hit nothing except at almost point-blank range.

"If you were struck by a jingal ball, you'd be badly hurt," a sailor observed. "But the chance of that happening was a slight one. . . ."

No matter how long the odds, there was always the possibility that a ball would find its mark. This happened to Private Dennis Hanrahan, a marine off the *Benecia,* who should have been up front with Tilton but was serving with a platoon of sailors due to an error in boat assignments. Because of the mixup, Hanrahan had come ashore with Wheeler's

men instead of with Tilton's. At any rate, he was hit in the head with a jingal ball and killed instantly, the first American fatality.

Moments after Hanrahan's death, Lieutenant Mead's battery ranged in on the Koreans. A salvo of four guns dropped the shells squarely in the midst of the enemy's close-packed ranks.

As the shells exploded, the attack shuddered to a stop. Four more shells came crashing down; men were blown to bits, killed, or horribly wounded by the impact. Shrieking in terror, the Koreans broke and ran, scattering wildly as the guns continued playing havoc among them. Back to the ridges they fled, and over the opposite side, followed by a rain of shells and bullets.

The jubilant Americans could barely be restrained from pursuing them, but Wheeler did not want to waste time or men in chasing a beaten force. His orders had been to clear out the strongpoints protecting Fort du Coude. With the Korean attack beaten off, he began moving his men against those objectives.

The fighting was brief. A round or two from a fieldpiece usually routed the foe from a particular bastion. The demoralized enemy fled to Fort du Coude, and the Americans took one target after another without firing a shot.

The defenders gave the sailors less trouble than did the rough terrain. But about 2 P.M. Wheeler's force ran into bitter resistance at the biggest and last redoubt. The Koreans holding it had two good pieces of artillery which they used with skill and exceptional marksmanship. The only approach to the redoubt, which was called the Devil's Nest, ran through a narrow defile several hundred yards long that led straight to the bastion. The enemy's guns were well-emplaced on the rampart and sited to cover the mouth of the defile.

Every time Wheeler's men started to move through the narrow passageway, the guns would open up and send shells screaming the length of the ravine. This forced the Americans to advance by crawling, but a sniper hidden somewhere on the wall of the Devil's Nest also covered the passage exit.

Armed with a fine modern rifle, the sniper was a superb marksman. Anyone who reached the head of the passageway came into the rifleman's sights. He soon sent a man scurrying for cover. The sniper's position was cleverly concealed, and he used cartridges with smokeless powder so that his precise location could not be pinpointed.

For some time after the battle it was rumored that the marksman was a British soldier of fortune who had roamed to Korea and gained the favor of Prince

Tai-Wun. However, his identity has remained a mystery throughout the years.

When he found that his men could not storm the bastion, Wheeler decided to employ different tactics and abandoned the idea of a frontal assault. Leaving a few men in the passage to keep the foe busy, Wheeler led the rest of his command in a wide-flanking march to get behind the Devil's Nest. His strategy was sound, but Wheeler ran into trouble trying to carry it out.

Seeking a route that would take him to the rear of the Devil's Nest, Wheeler brought the men into a canyon which led them through a confusing maze of rocks, boulders, dead-end arroyos, and deep dry stream beds. All around, they could hear the sounds of battle, the crack of rifles, the *crump* of bursting shells, but no matter what direction he took, Wheeler was unable to find a way out of the blind alley into which he had wandered.

While much of the landing force's left wing was stumbling about among Kanghwa's rocky labyrinths, the American right wing had a hot fight on its hands. Early in the morning, Casey's units had linked up with Tilton's marines, but the ground mist kept them from taking any major action.

When the mist burned off, Casey maneuvered his force of bluejackets and leathernecks into a position from which to attack Fort du Coude. It was planned that Wheeler would make a coordinated assault from the left; but as the morning progressed and the left wing seemed to have stalled after beating off the Korean counterattack, Casey decided to move on his own.

By semaphore, he signaled the *Monocacy* to shell the citadel where General Wo-Pei's flag still defiantly flew. Casey had led his men to a hilltop some four hundred yards from Fort du Coude and there they crouched as the gunboat's shells slammed into the fortress.

The fieldpieces attached to Casey's command were hauled to the top of the hill from where they joined in pounding Fort du Coude. The Americans had no way of telling just how effective the shelling was. After a while, the target was almost completely obscured by smoke. No breeze stirred, and in the oppressive heat the waiting men suffered great discomfort.

About 1:30 P.M., after an hour-long bombardment, the *Monocacy* signaled that she was running low on ammunition and must cease firing. A similar situation developed with the field artillery. Lieutenant A. S. Snow, commanding the four-gun battery in Casey's sector, reported that he had to conserve his remaining shells.

As Casey later noted, "With the guns forced to desist from firing, the hot potato was passed to me and I dared not drop it. . . . If that fort was to be taken, my men and I would have to do it. . . . I would have preferred a more prolonged bombardment; indeed one so intensive that it would have caused the enemy to run up a flag of surrender. However, that was not to be. We would have to take the fort by storm. . . . I had no recourse but to order my men to the attack, without knowing whether or not the shelling had weakened the foe. It was not an easy decision for me to make. . . . However, I could not keep my men on that hillside indefinitely, and although I did not know what had become of Wheeler on the left, I ordered the charge. . . ."

A bugle sounded the quick, stirring notes that electrified every man who heard them. All the ranks of the 350 sailors and marines poised on that hillside raised the cry "Go get 'em!"

As the bugle shrilled on and on, the bluejackets and leathernecks, with fixed bayonets, dashed down the hill. Leading them was Lieutenant Hugh McKee, an officer off the *Palos*, whose father had been killed at the head of such a charge during the battle of Shiloh in the Civil War.

Fort du Coude stood on a steep, rocky hillside just

opposite the one the Americans had occupied. At the bottom of the slope was a ravine into which the Americans came sliding and tumbling. Panting from their downhill dash, Casey's men began scrambling up the hill to reach Fort du Coude.

When the American attack got under way, General Wo-Pei sent soldiers to man a low parapet that formed the outer wall of the fort. Five or six hundred Koreans took up positions on that wall or in the courtyard behind it. As many others went to the main walls of the citadel some fifty yards behind the outer parapet.

Although the *Monocacy* had battered the fort and the fieldpieces had caused some destruction, casualties were light and the bastion remained in good order.

When the Koreans took up their posts, they began the same wailing chant that had been heard the night before. At intervals, the chanting died out and the men shouted in unison, "Death to the foreign dogs!" Then their mournful keening was resumed.

Wo-Pei's soldiers on the outerworks fired at the Americans clambering out of the ravine below. The jingals did not hamper the men awkwardly grabbling their way up the steep slope.

"SOMEHOW, I FEEL ASHAMED..." 13

"THE MOST DIFFICULT PART OF THE ENTIRE AFFAIR
was the long climb uphill to reach the fort," a sailor
off the *Alaska* wrote to his brother. "When I die, I
know I'm going to heaven, because I spent my time
in hell during that awful ordeal. . . . Imagine, if
you can, inching up what seemed like a sheer preci-
pice. . . . Encumbered by a rifle, weighted down
by a pack and ammunition belt . . . I climbed. . . .
The sun turned that airless ravine into a bake oven
. . . and then, somehow, we were at the top . . .
and then we fought. . . ."

The young sailor off the *Alaska* was not exaggerating when he equated the climb out of the ravine with hell. No man who endured that experience was ever likely to forget it. Even under perfect conditions it would have been a difficult accomplishment.

There was neither a trail nor a path to follow. The hillside was rock and shale which the rains and snows of centuries had eroded smooth and slippery. A man had no handhold; he had to find a niche and somehow pull himself up.

Some men lost their rifles on the climb, others narrowly escaped slipping down into the ravine. Ahead, they looked upward into the belching muzzles of the jingals, feeling the sting of powder, deafened by the noise, flinching at the whining ricochet of the bullets.

Grimly, resolutely, they crept on, because it was the only way they could go. Here, one could not turn back; so they crawled, like human flies, up that cruel slope, with hands torn and bleeding, uniforms ripped, weapons scraping and clattering against the rocks.

At last a handful of Americans was at the crest. The first man to make it was Seth Allen, a sailor off the *Colorado*. But before he could take a step, he fell riddled by a dozen jingal balls.

Hoarsely shouting "Forward! Forward!" Lieutenant Hugh McKee scaled the parapet, a revolver clutched in his hand. No sooner had he gone over the wall than a dozen Koreans rushed him. They impaled him on their spears and hacked at him with swords. McKee fell, bleeding from many wounds, and died on the wall. Right behind him came a rush of Americans led by Lieutenant Commander Schley, who had a revolver in each hand, pumping bullets left and right.

In moments, the wall and the courtyard were the scene of swirling, maniacal hand-to-hand fighting. The Americans used revolvers, bayonets, rifle butts, and cutlasses while the Koreans fought back with swords, spears, and their clumsy muskets. In some places fists, knives, and stones were used. The soldiers of the Hermit Kingdom had little chance against the bigger, stronger Americans.

Once the bluejackets and leathernecks had breached the walls, Wo-Pei's men could not drive them back. The general watched the struggle in the courtyard for a few minutes and then bolted out of the fort through a rear exit, followed by his aides and scores of panic-stricken soldiers.

When they reached the open, the fleeing Koreans were spotted by observers on the *Monocacy*. The ship's guns killed and wounded many of them. The gunboat kept firing until all her shells were gone. As the Koreans ran, blindly seeking some place of sanctuary, Wheeler's lost detachment unexpectedly came out of a pass into which they had blundered.

The Americans were as surprised as the foe. Wheeler had been vainly trying to get behind the Devil's Nest; instead, he was to the rear of Fort du Coude, athwart the enemy's escape route. A maneuver that had begun in bumbling error was accidentally turned into a stroke of strategic genius which brought much praise for Wheeler.

Recovering from the initial shock of barging head on into hundreds of Koreans, Wheeler's men sent a withering fire into the unlucky enemy soldiers, causing numerous casualties. However, many hundreds of Koreans made their escape, including the men who had defended the Devil's Nest.

General Wo-Pei and his staff were among those who got away. The general reached Seoul that evening and gave his version of the day's events to Prince Tai-Wun. He must have delivered a highly self-laudatory report, for the Prince treated him as a winner, not as a loser.

A few days later, the general was presented with a medal and a jeweled dagger as a token of the esteem in which the ruler held him. Wo-Pei was obviously a better politician than he was a soldier. He was hailed in the capital as a hero and the "Savior

of the Country." By royal edict, June 11 was hence-
forth to be celebrated as a fete day to honor Wo-Pei
and the "Tiger Warriors of Kanghwa."

The complete American victory evoked little joy
among the men who had gained it. Their triumph
seemed hollow to them. The sailors and marines
were aware that they had beaten an enemy lacking
training and modern weapons. The Korean summer
heat, the terrain, the insects, all had been more difficult to cope with than had the foe.

The Koreans had fought with futile courage in
Fort du Coude. Their brave stand brought praise
from the Americans. "Had those people been properly armed, I believe the outcome might have been
different," declared an officer off the *Colorado*.
"They have spirit and the hearts of fighters."

In the battle for Fort du Coude alone, the Koreans
had suffered more than two hundred killed and many
wounded. Staring at the corpses strewn about the
courtyard, a marine said, "Somehow, I feel ashamed
of what we have done here today. It all seems without purpose."

Long after the battle, another leatherneck who
had been in it stated, "Of late, I have given thought
to that time we stormed the forts on Kanghwa Island. I now believe we were wrong in attacking the
Koreans. They had done us no harm. It was their

right and duty to keep trespassers out, and no matter how we may wrap the package—we were trespassers."

But on higher political levels, the ethics and mo-
rality of the American punitive action were given
little importance. Rodgers and Low were swayed
by the current thinking of that day. It was an era of
freewheeling imperialism; nations were chauvinistic
and out for mercantile supremacy. The flag was the
national symbol, and any insult to it had to be
avenged by force if no other form of satisfaction
could be obtained. The small countries of the world
were at the complete mercy of the big and the strong.
Few bothered to question the dictum that "might
makes right."

However, the episode of the forts of Kanghwa
Island left a bitter aftertaste with the Americans.
The unpalatable task of burying the dead remained
for the victors.

Mass graves were dug outside Fort du Coude,
which was renamed Fort McKee for the fallen American officer. McKee, Hanrahan, and Allen were in-
terred with full military honors in the soil upon
which they had lost their lives. The grim work was
done by dusk of that bloody Sunday.

The burial parties had counted 365 Korean bodies;
another 100 enemy wounded were given first aid and

then left to their own resources. It was rumored,
but not confirmed, that about 50 Koreans had com-
mitted suicide by jumping off a high cliff on another
part of Kanghwa Island. According to this story, the
men had killed themselves in penance for the dis-
grace of defeat.

The truth of the suicide tale could not be ascer-
tained, but that was the least pressing problem facing Commander Blake when he came ashore after
Fort du Coude, or McKee, had been secured.

14 "WELL DONE, ALL HANDS!"

SEIZING THE FORTS AND DRIVING OUT THE KOREANS were only a part of Commander Blake's orders. He now had to level the strongholds, spike the guns, and blow up all magazines and arsenals.

Razing those forts was easier said than done. The thick walls had withstood wind and weather for centuries and were not likely to be blasted down by the quantity of explosives the commander had available.

After a talk with his officers, Blake decided that the best he could do was to destroy magazines, arsenals, and guns. Because it was too late to begin the demolitions that day, he ordered the landing force to spend the night in Fort McKee. He also wanted to show the Koreans that the Americans could hold what they had captured.

"We'd have been in a tight spot had the Koreans mounted a counterattack that night," an officer recalled. "The *Monocacy* was out of shells, the *Palos* barely managed to keep herself afloat with pumps going full blast. The river water had seeped into her ammunition locker and ruined all the shells stored there. Our men were physically worn. Many had only a few cartridges left. If the enemy had hit us in the darkness, I think very few of us would have lived to see the dawn. . . ."

But the demoralized Koreans made no forays, and the Americans passed another tense night on Kanghwa Island. Fort McKee had little to offer in the way of comfort for either officers or enlisted men. Everyone bedded down as best he could after another meal of hardtack and water.

Once again rain fell and a chill wind whistled in from the river. The sailors and marines huddled against the damp night air which contrasted so sharply with the fierce heat of the day.

Somehow, the night dragged by; the hours seemed interminable to the men in the fort. Those unlucky

enough to draw guard duty peered out into a black-
ness unrelieved by a moonbeam or the faintest star-
light.

"The darkness was incredible," a marine recalled.
"We were in a deep void. This was the pit and we
were at its bottom. I walked sentry go from two
o'clock in the morning until four. We called it the
graveyard watch. I spent two hours of unrelieved
terror. . . ."

Eventually, even the longest night ended. The
Americans were awakened before daybreak. Another
breakfast of hardtack and water was eaten. The
demolition teams, selected the night before, went
out to mine the arsenals and magazines.

Wrecking crews spiked the guns. Everything
breakable was demolished or put to the torch. By
midmorning, all was ready for the work of destruction. Down at the river, steam launches towing boats
in their wake put in to shore, waiting to embark the
landing force.

About 11:30 A.M. the American withdrawal from
Kanghwa Island got under way. First, the fieldpieces were manhandled down to the shore, this
time on solid ground all the way, hauled aboard
boats, and lashed in place. Then, platoon by platoon,
the sailors entered the boats. They were followed

by the marines. Last came the demolitionists sprinting breathlessly to the beach after lighting delayed-action fuses.

When these men were safely aboard, the launches pulled out, with the long lines of boats trailing after. The procession had not gone very far from shore when the explosions began going off, one after another, like a mammoth Fourth of July fireworks display.

Sheets of red and orange flames, followed by teeth-jarring detonations, came in rapid succession from where the mines had been planted. Rocks and earth were hurled into the air. The last of the explosions took place in Fort McKee. The men looking on from the river had to shield their eyes from the huge sheets of fire that shot skyward above the citadel.

Searing heat from furiously burning fires on shore was felt by the men in the boats even when they reached midstream where the *Monocacy* lay at anchor. From the gunboat's deck, Commander Blake waved the launches to continue downriver to Boisée Anchorage.

With the crippled *Palos*, listing badly to port, limping in the rear, and the steam launch *Weehawken* up front, followed by the *Monocacy* and the launches hauling the boats, the punitive expedition drew away from Kanghwa Island, over which black smoke clouds arched mutely, indicating the ruin and devastation that had occurred there.

The men in the boats who so lately had fought on the ravaged island turned to stare back until they rounded a bend which hid Kanghwa from view. Only the columns of smoke rising in oily pillars remained in sight.

The convoy reached Boisée Anchorage and the main fleet by 2 P.M. Signal flags reading: "Well Done, All Hands!" flew from the flagship.

The marines and sailors of the landing force were returned to their ships where hot water for bathing and hot meals had been prepared. Admiral Rodgers declared a day off for the fleet, and the men had nothing to do but eat, clean up, loaf, sleep, and swap tall tales about their recent adventures.

The admiral prepared a congratulatory message which was read to all personnel by commanding officers. Rodgers stated in General Order #32: "To one and all the Commander in Chief expresses his thanks and justly feels proud in commanding such a fine body of officers and enlisted men."

"ON TO SEOUL!"

15

AFTER THE EXPEDITIONARY FORCE HAD RETURNED, Admiral Rodgers and Ambassador Low began to have second thoughts about the wisdom of Operation Punishment. Even after long conferences with Blake, Kimberley, and other officers, they could not decide on a policy for the immediate future.

While their leaders debated, the enlisted men passed the time by spreading scuttlebutt. According to the grapevine, the fleet would be resupplied for an attack directly on Seoul. The Korean capital was

143

to be burned, according to the rumormongers. This tale passed from one ship to the other until it blanketed the entire squadron. "On to Seoul!" the men gibed. Signalmen wigwagged the phrase to each other. It became a comic line in the fleet. When an enlisted man was assigned to an unpleasant chore, he would cry, "On to Seoul!" Those words served as a substitute for rawer, earthier language.

Beneath the constant use of the expression ran a current of anxiety. The men worried that an attack on Seoul might actually be in the offing. Even the dimmest possibility of carrying out such a drastic move affected the men's morale. The sailors and marines who would have to do the fighting did not relish the idea.

However, there was little chance that the "brass" was seriously contemplating such a step. No one knew better than they how impractical it was. Both the *Monocacy* and the *Palos* needed overhauling; indeed, the latter required major repairs.

The Americans had neither the men, ships, nor armament to undertake a drive for Seoul. The best he could do, Rodgers felt, was to pull out and return to Woosing. Every day he dallied longer in Korean waters the fleet was endangered by shortages. Food stocks were running low. Ammunition was badly depleted. Medical stores were getting short. All his experience and instinct told Rodgers that he must leave at once.

However, there were political factors which had to be considered. Should the Americans withdraw so precipitously, the Koreans would look on their departure as weakness. Ambassador Low pointed out that the Kanghwa affair had been undertaken to convince the Koreans that the United States was strong.

"Most assuredly we will be unable to bring the Prince to a conference table should we now falter or hesitate," Low declared. "We must be firm and unyielding at this juncture."

Although Low stood virtually alone in opposing a withdrawal, his will prevailed. As the ranking official of the United States government, the ambassador's decision outweighed the rest; he was the policy maker.

Notes were exchanged with the Koreans during the week following the Battle of Kanghwa. The Koreans were enraged over what had taken place, and their attitude daily grew more intractable and bellicose. On June 19 a message from Seoul advised Rodgers that Prince Tai-Wun had taken a solemn vow never to deal with the Americans "except at sword point."

The Prince affirmed this pledge by having erected in Seoul's main square a monument to those who had fallen while defending Kanghwa's forts. On this stone tablet were to be engraved the Prince's prayer for the dead and a dire curse upon all foreigners, particularly Americans. The anathema also applied to any Korean who might betray the nation by having dealings with "foreign devils" for "any cause or reason." (The memorial remained until 1950 when it was destroyed in the street fighting that wracked Seoul during the Korean War.)

Despite the negative tone of the messages from Seoul, Low continued to press for a meeting with Tai-Wun. In an effort to show "good faith," the ambassador offered to pay reparations for the damage done to the Kanghwa forts and an additional sum to compensate the families of the dead. This proposal had an opposite effect on Korean authorities than the one Low had anticipated. It stirred them to even greater wrath and indignation. In a stinging rejoinder, a high Korean official sneered, "We put no price on human lives! How can you evaluate a person's monetary worth? One may buy a bullock—but not a human being! Or is that a custom in your land? Do murderers repay the families of victims in cash?"

As the days rolled along, it was clear that there would be no trade treaty with Seoul or, for that matter, an agreement about shipwrecked merchant mariners. If any hope had ever existed, the American action at Kanghwa had ruined it.

Gloom enshrouded the American fleet moored at Boisée Anchorage. Day after day, the waiting became more irksome. Morale aboard the ships deteriorated. Discipline began breaking down as the men objected to the continued stay with food rations cut, no shore leave, and nothing to do but routine tasks. During the last week in June, a spell of tropical weather gripped the region. The temperature rose to more than one hundred degrees and remained at that level twenty-four hours a day.

The ships were motionless on the glassy smooth water of the anchorage. Not a breeze rippled the mirror-like surface. The men of the fleet suffered great discomfort. The fo'c'sles were intolerably hot and airless. Even the officers' quarters were sweatboxes. No rain fell to ease the heat spell. The Americans grumbled at their chores. To make matters worse, the ice in the ships' cold-storage lockers melted, and perishable foodstuff spoiled.

As one sailor recorded in his diary: "I am reminded of the Ancient Mariner. . . . Here we are as idle as painted ships on a painted ocean, the way he was in Coleridge's poem. . . ."

The sun rose like a red fireball and went down the same way, a giant, unblinking red eye, searing the earth. The dry period brought on a fresh crisis for the Americans. Ever since the fleet had come to Boisée Anchorage, details had gone out daily from each vessel anchored there to refill water casks from springs ashore.

Due to the hot weather and lack of rain, once-abundant springs had fallen to a mere trickle. Water sources close at hand were dwindling, and the Americans dared not venture farther inland to search for water because they feared the Koreans might ambush water parties in that heavily wooded region.

At last, realizing that nothing further could be gained by staying, Ambassador Low gave Rodgers permission to withdraw. It was announced to the fleet that the ships were hauling anchor on the morning flood tide, Monday, July 3. When this decision was read to the assembled crews on Sunday, the cheering, applauding men broke ranks and cavorted about the decks. Their ordeal was coming to an end. The three-week period in Boisée Anchorage had turned into an endurance test for the Americans.

In a report to the Secretary of the Navy, Admiral Rodgers stated: "It is my measured opinion that no purpose would have been fulfilled in holding our

position. . . . I am convinced that the morale of
our crews was at a breaking point and that serious
disciplinary problems would have arisen had we not
withdrawn from Boisée Anchorage. . . ."

Before final sailing orders were issued, the five
shipwrecked Koreans who had been carried from
Woosing were set ashore.

On Monday morning, July 3, 1871, at 10 A.M., the
Colorado hoisted the signal "All ships sortie!" In
single column with the *Monocacy* to the fore and
the *Palos* limping off the port beam of the *Colorado,*
the five American ships sailed out of Boisée Anchorage on a course for Woosing.

Lookouts on the ships noticed that "hundreds"
of Koreans—men, women, and children—lined the
shore to witness the departure. No sound came from
the onlookers; nothing but a sense of implacable
hatred rose like a foul miasma from the silent
spectators.

"We could not see the faces of the people on
land," an *Alaska* crewman recalled. "But we felt
their eyes burning into us. Perhaps this was only
imagination. Perhaps we only guessed their hatred
because each man felt guilty for those we had killed
on Kanghwa. . . . I remember, as we were clearing the headland, I heard a baby's wailing. That
thin cry was as if amplified a thousandfold in my

ears. . . . It seemed to me to symbolize the desolation and terror we were leaving behind us. . . . It was the last sound I heard in Korea. . . ."

"THIS EXPEDITION REFLECTS NO GLORY..." 16

AMBASSADOR LOW WAS ONLY A FAIR DIPLOMAT, BUT a splendid politician. He never allowed an opponent to believe that he had acted out of weakness. Indeed, he had developed the ability to make it seem that his every move was somehow a blow at an antagonist.

Shortly before the American fleet lifted anchor, Low sent ashore a message which stated: "We are not retreating. We are withdrawing to some other point on the coast of Korea or China to await instructions from our government. . . ." He also included an implied threat of even greater force if American merchant vessels or their crews were mistreated in the future.

While Low had no authority to sound such a warning, he did so in the belief that the Koreans must be made to fear a massive reprisal if they repeated the *General Sherman* case with another vessel. The ambassador felt that the mere possibility of American retribution would make the Koreans act with restraint.

Under the circumstances, Ambassador Low and Admiral Rodgers were convinced that their mission to Korea had turned out to be a complete failure. They had come to negotiate a treaty and instead fought a bloody battle with no tangible results other than lives lost and property destroyed. The trade treaty was as remote as ever after the Battle of Kanghwa. Despite the threat of force, there was no guarantee that shipwrecked sailors would receive any better treatment in the future.

The attack on the Kanghwa forts soon came under sharp criticism in Washington. Senators and congressmen denounced the action. Low and Rodgers were called before a congressional committee investigating the incident. Low defended the decision, but his reasons were flat and trite. He said: "The chastisement of the Koreans has done good. . . . It has convinced all nations that insults to the United States and her flag will not be allowed to go un-redressed. . . . This has increased respect for us in the Far East. . . ."

But Low must have known better even as he was mouthing those dreary phrases. Because the American ships had dallied so long in Korean waters after the battle, the reports about it that reached China and Japan were unfavorable to the United States.

Chinese traders had brought back from Seoul the first accounts of what had taken place on Kanghwa. Since the only version they had was from Korean sources, their stories were highly colored and in-accurate. According to the traders, the American ships had been badly damaged; the landing force on Kanghwa, practically annihilated.

It was a defeat worse than that suffered by the French in 1866. Initially these reports were greeted with skepticism in Woosing and elsewhere. But as days and weeks passed without the American fleet returning, some credence was given to the stories of a disaster.

By July 7, when Rodgers' squadron put in at Woosing, another yarn was going the rounds to the effect that the ships that had been observed head-ing for port were loaded with wounded men.

The foreign colony in Woosing decided to do something to help the "suffering" Americans. As the ships appeared on the horizon, the docks were lined with ambulances for the wounded. All available doctors and nurses were waiting. A corps of volunteer stretcher bearers had been formed.

A German sloop went out to meet the Americans. When the ships were sighted, the German raised the signal "Accept our condolences. What help do you need?"

The *Colorado,* which had received the message, raised her own flags to request that the German signal be repeated. When this was done, Admiral Rodgers suddenly realized what the German meant. He replied: "Require no help. Please get out of my way so I can land."

To offset the impression that the Americans had suffered a defeat, Rodgers ordered every ship to break out victory signals. All hands were to stand in formation on the main deck. The *Colorado*'s small band was to furnish "spirited music." "We're coming into port like victors!" Rodgers signaled his fleet.

The triumphant style of the American arrival dispelled the rumors that they had met with disaster. But the negative stories still persisted. For the next days, liberty parties off American ships fought pitched battles with British and German sailors who ragged them for being whipped by the Koreans.

In the last analysis, the victory at Kanghwa proved to be no victory at all. It remained what it always was—a sordid, tragic incident. In the words of a United States senator of that day: "This expedition reflects no glory on the United States. . . ."

Eleven years after the Battle of Kanghwa, the Koreans finally negotiated limited trade treaties with Western nations. The last country Seoul signed with was the United States.

Americans returned to Korea again in 1945 when World War II ended; but this time the American troops were greeted with cheers and flowers. Once more, in 1950, American fighting men trod Korean soil, when the Republic of North Korea, abetted by the Soviet Union and Communist China, attacked South Korea. Not only Americans, but thousands of men from Great Britain, Turkey, Greece, and other countries came to the aid of the South Korean Republic under the banner of the United Nations.

In July 1953 that war ended in a stalemated armistice. Fifteen years later, in 1968, Americans were once again embroiled in Korea. The U.S.S. *Pueblo,* a United States naval "observation" ship sailing off the coast of North Korea, was seized by the North Koreans. Imprisoned and tortured for nearly a year, the Americans were finally released in late 1968, but the *Pueblo* remained in North Korean hands.

The United States entered the Hermit Kingdom nearly a century ago, and since that distant day, has been deeply involved with the ancient country once called Chosen—the Land of the Morning Calm —now known as Korea, where calm has long been absent.

BIBLIOGRAPHY

I used diaries, memoirs, ships' logs and official reports in my research. *The Annual Report of the Secretary of the Navy, 1871,* which is not available to general readers, contains all the original reports and related correspondence concerning this incident.

Dudley W. Knox's *A History of the United States Navy* covers the events of June 1871 in Korea. *Rear Admiral John Rodgers, 1812–1882,* by Robert E. Johnson, is an admirable biography which covers the incident in depth.

However, the finest sources of material were the

newspapers of that time. *The New York Times* and the *New York Herald* had good news coverage of the episode. Illustrated papers such as *Harper's Weekly, Frank Leslie's Illustrated Weekly* and the *London Illustrated News* gave the Korean clash wide coverage enlivened by splendid steel engravings of the ships and portraits of leading personalities.